OMG That's Me!

OMG That's Me!

**Bipolar Disorder, Depression, Anxiety,
Panic Attacks, and More...**

Dave Mowry

ISBN-13: 9781546356158
ISBN-10: 1546356150

To Joanne Doan and Shane Furgal of *bp Magazine for Bipolar*, for giving me the opportunity to write about my experiences and touch tens of thousands of lives and for the ability to share them in this book.

To the National Alliance on Mental Illness of Clackamas County, Oregon, for understanding, supporting, and helping me move from my dark days into the light.

Acknowledgments

I want to express my special thanks to Joanne Doan and Shane Furgal from bp Magazine for Bipolar for their support and guidance.

Thank you to my amazing friend and best-selling author Julie Fast. Thank you, Julie, for your friendship and support.

Very important—I want to thank the people who had enough confidence in me to make major contributions of money and time to my Kickstarter campaign to help pay for editing, formatting, design, and so on. Thank you, Jeff Caton, Heather Mowry, and Julie Fast.

I want to recognize Judy Winter for her acceptance and support during my dark days and for first telling me that my story was worth sharing.

And finally, thank you from the bottom of my heart to my wife Heather for staying with me during the dark days. And to Heather, Brooke, Meghan, and David Mowry for supporting me while I so publically tell our story.

Contents

Introduction

*B*ipolar disorder is thought to be mania and depression alternating back and forth, with thoughts of grandiosity alternating with emptiness and despair. It is this. But it is also much more.

Kay Baily Jameson in her book *An Unquiet Mind* expertly describes the effects of mania and depression on her life, helping untold numbers of people. She shows that one can go through the extremes and come out the other side resilient and productive.

William Styron's book *Darkness Visible* had a powerful influence on me. His memoir is the best description of depression I have read. I strongly recommend it to anyone who wants to know what it is truly like to be caught in the grips of depression.

Bipolar disorder is much more than these symptoms. In my awareness and writing, and the thousands of responses I have had to it, in my ability to see myself for who I am, and in my being in touch with my life's experiences, I find myself to be a kind of bipolar everyman. Let me explain what I mean.

In truth, bipolar disorder is a combination of symptoms that manifest themselves in unique ways, sometimes alone but often together. There is anxiety, which has haunted me since I was twelve. While the mania and depression would come and go, more often and more intense as I have grown older, the extreme anxiety I experienced was constant. It was awful, dreadful, and miserable.

Bipolar disorder is also constant conversations in my brain. I get distracted by another thought every thirty seconds or so. I have my favorite song, "Doctor My Eyes" by Jackson Browne, a song I have never been able to listen to all the way through. I feel the song and its powerful impact on me, but if I try to sing along, I can't remember the words. And I have listened to this song at least a hundred times.

Bipolar disorder is obsessive-compulsive thoughts and behaviors. This is not a major portion of the illness for me, but it is there, and I experience it daily. Every morning when I take my meds and make my coffee, I try to be most efficient. I count my steps from the coffee pot to the refrigerator. Four steps back and forth. From the sink it is two steps from where I keep my medicine. I have it down to twelve steps to make my coffee and take my meds. It is always twelve steps. And I always count each step.

Bipolar disorder is racing thoughts. This is different than constant conversations in my head. My racing thoughts are usually negative and usually the same thought over and over and over again. I can't get it out of my head. It is exhausting.

Bipolar disorder is memory loss and the inability to remember things a minute or two after I read, see, or hear them. It is long-term memory loss. It is forgetting experiences and making the same mistake over and over again.

Bipolar disorder is ADD. I can't assemble anything, even when I'm trying to follow directions. I look at them, and they make no sense. I can't connect the dots. I can't focus. The feeling inside is that I have to escape from this task that is causing incredible anxiety. One more minute creates a major panic attack that incapacitates me; sometimes this incapacitation lasts for days. Escape is my only option.

Bipolar disorder is the impact of the memory loss, ADHD, dread, anxiety, racing thoughts, depression, mania, panic attacks, and more. Bipolar disorder is suffering in silence and mourning the lost years.

Bipolar disorder is misreading situations and people and constantly checking to see if things are as they seem to be.

To understand bipolar disorder is to understand all these symptoms and the effects they have on the lives of those of us who have this illness.

This book is about the impact of the symptoms of bipolar disorder on my life. And in turn what I write about relates to all people with some or all of these symptoms and to all those who know, love, or provide mental-health services to us.

Some of these chapters will speak to you more than others. I have laid out the chapters with a purpose, but it doesn't matter if you read them in order. What is important is to read them all. When you have read them all, you will be drawn back to the ones that speak loudest to you. This book is meant to be a companion—a book you will come back to again and again.

The comments I include tell the stories of other people's lives. I recommend reading these as well. I have edited some of these comments for grammar and length but never to change their messages. Most of them are printed as they were originally written, typos and all. These comments are a quick read.

Each chapter is written with absolute honesty. Nothing is made up except for the man I talk to about a conversation I had with a stranger about five things that people with bipolar disorder can do to improve their lives. The stranger's voice is mine.

For each chapter, I go back to my experiences and relive them. This was both incredibly painful and healing. Putting these experiences down on the page was scary. This is me being completely open about my life with mental illness. This is me no longer suffering in silence or hiding in the shadows.

I hide nothing in order to tell the real story about mental illness. People with these symptoms will read this book and say, "Yes, yes, yes. That's it. That's me. Finally there are words for my experiences, pain, loss, fears, and hopes." They will have another tool with which to describe their symptoms to family, health-care providers, and friends.

Providers of mental-health services will read this book and say, "Wow, this will help me in my practice." The *DSM-5* (which is the standard classification of mental disorders used by mental-health professionals) describes mental illness in medical terms. Reading this book, providers will really see inside.

Family and friends will read this book and come away with understanding, compassion, and empathy.

Reading these chapters will uncover a moving combination of feelings. Let yourself be immersed in them. Let them out. Let the healing begin.

1 | Obsessive Thoughts and Behavior

One thing we are doing makes us feel good at first. Since it feels good, we want to do more of it. Soon we are thinking of nothing else. Our normal daily activities get left by the wayside, and soon all we are thinking about is the one thing we want to do.

~

*B*ipolar disorder is recognized as mania and depression and usually anxiety. One area of bipolar disorder not usually talked about is obsessive thoughts and behavior.

The lucky ones recognize obsessive behavior early and identify what it is that makes us obsessive. Most of us, however, get stuck in our obsessive brains. We know that something is not right, but we don't know what. Rational thought seems to be pushed aside.

The obsession comes with balance, mania, or hypomania. We have energy and are doing things. Hopefully we are accomplishing things that need to be done. But then there is trouble.

One thing we are doing makes us feel good at first. Since it feels good, we want to do more of it. Soon we are thinking of nothing else. Our normal daily activities get left by the wayside, and soon all we are thinking about is the one thing we want to do.

From here it is not pretty. We think about it when we go to bed. Obsessing about it at night keeps us from falling asleep. We wake up tired and thinking about our obsession in the morning. We know there are other things that need to be done at home, at work, and with friends and family. We try to think about these things. But our minds keep going back to the obsession.

This is happening to me now. I recently started gardening. I enjoy it until it is all I am thinking about and all that I am doing.

This is the toughest blog I have written. I usually look forward to writing and sharing my experiences with you. But today my mind is in another place.

I know I am obsessing in the garden when I keep having the same thoughts over and over again. I will go from one thing to another and then come full circle. I will do this over and over because I want to keep gardening even though there is nothing left to do.

I find myself just sitting and looking at the plants for a long while. Then I see a stem that needs to be trimmed, and I do it. Then I look for more stems. Then I check the water for the fourth time. I am being pulled to stay there. So I sit.

I try to distract myself and pick up that book that I started reading six months ago and am only on chapter 3 of. However, I can't concentrate. My mind drifts back to the garden, and I am drawn to it again.

I like watching basketball on TV. Usually I have no problem sitting down to watch a game. After the game starts, I am into it—until the first timeout and commercial. Then my mind goes back to the garden. It is not that I have to do something specific. It is just that I can't stop thinking about it.

At this point, the obsession doesn't feel good. It feels like a flaw, and I feel guilty for the things I have neglected.

But still I can't do these things. At halftime of the game, I am back in the garden. I am looking at plants for the tenth time today.

Today is my blog day, so I set my alarm with two reminders. I wanted to ignore them and keep staring at plants. I knew I was wasting my time, but I could not stop. After the second reminder, I knew that I needed to start the blog in order to meet my deadline.

By writing, I am accomplishing something. It feels good, but I still have that gnawing, negative feeling in the pit of my stomach. I wonder what will happen when I am done. Will I be drawn back to the garden, or will I put in that load of laundry that I have been putting off for three days?

I know I need to do more than watch plants grow. I know I will feel guilty if I continue to ignore important parts of my life for the sake of an obsession. I'm good at feeling guilty. I have lots of experience with it.

So as I sign off, I don't know what is going to happen. Will the good feeling from writing carry over so I can do other things that need doing and that I will feel good about if I do them? Or will these obsessive thoughts and actions win out? Now is the time to get control of my thoughts. I hope I can.

"Dave…just so excited I found this today! Right now I'm obsessed w everything having to do w my hamster, including sneaking in his room in the dark at night to see what he's doing. Hiding and watching for hours. This is in the middle of the night. I am always exhausted. But other thoughts happen at evening every night! Thanks. I don't feel alone and so crazy."

"I obsess over horrible things…things I can't get out of my head; they consume me. I get the compulsive cleaning where I start by emptying the dishwasher then end up with it taken apart cleaning the inside out and any area I can unscrew to take apart and clean… then it's on to the fridge, cupboards and drawers. Soon the day is gone and that's all I've accomplished. But it's nothing in comparison to the negative obsessions. I feel that my husband hates me, that he talks about me behind my back…I search his messages on his PC and his e-mail. I'm paranoid that he wants someone else or just wants me gone. I'm literally driving myself mad…he knows I go through his stuff; I think he tries to understand, IDK. I know how destructive and unhealthy, let alone absolutely bonkers, this is in my own mind, yet I'm in utter lack of control of my racing, obsessive thoughts…it's hell…"

"Reading things here comforts me. I know why I obsess; my husband has a harder time…I don't obsess over an action; it's my thoughts…the older I get, the harder it is to initiate an action because I think it to death…like *I should start a garden. It would be healthy to obtain a hobby to consume some of my time.* But no gardening or hobbies…my mind goes back and forth on why it would or wouldn't work to the point that I'm sick of it but can't stop thinking about it and can't get up and do it. I've resorted to mind-numbing drugs just so I can function…I have literally sat in the same spot in my bed for months, unable to focus on anything productive."

"I do not seem to have one thing I'm obsessing over. But obsession is a part of my life. I do seem to have one argument in my head I'm replaying now. The silent discussion goes on in there constantly. The discussion becomes vocal when I am by myself. I have a day, maybe two, every couple of years when the inner dialogue stops. I always journal it. It feels like a burden lifted. It's not the 'voices in my head' kind of voices; it's just me, obsessing over some conversation or situation that I feel went awry. But I always know when there is something pulling at me because I cannot settle down to any of the things that usually soothe me like knitting, crochet tatting, some art, reading…nothing, not even the ability to escape into sleep. I keep organizing stuff to start a project or art piece, something, changing bags to carry it in but…then can settle to nothing. I'm pretty sure there is some obsessing going on somewhere that I'm subconsciously squashing; I just haven't caught hold of it yet. Thanks for the clue."

2 | Which Bipolar Me Is Going to Wake Up Today?

I don't know which bipolar me is going to wake up in the morning: the me that feels good or the me that is not sad but not motivated either. Then there is the depressed me. I wake up with negative thoughts. I sit on the couch doing nothing and look forward to a nap and then bed.

~

Today I woke up feeling good. I am active and having good thoughts. I realized this about mid-morning when I was standing in line at the pharmacy. I thought, *Wow, I feel good.* My next thought was not *Yay, I feel good.* My next thought was *Why am I realizing I feel good? Is it because this is such an unusual occurrence?*

I don't know which bipolar me is going to wake up in the morning: the me that feels good or the me that is not sad but not motivated either. Then there is the depressed me. I wake up with negative thoughts. I sit on the couch doing nothing and look forward to a nap and then bed.

Not knowing which me is going to wake up is hard. It is hard to make plans. It is hard on my wife. It is hard on my kids.

This has been going on since before I was diagnosed. Even with depression medication, I am still in a state of low-grade depression. This is my default mode. I get by. I can function around people. But I don't feel good. Feeling good is a rare occurrence for me, so rare that when it happens, I recognize the change.

Today I am trying to figure out why I am happy. Did I sleep particularly well last night? Did I eat more healthily than usual? Has something changed in my life? I do feel less stress today. Is this why I feel good? Is less stress why I am happy, or am I happy because I feel less stress?

I just don't know. Even as I explore why I feel good, I still feel good—frustrated but good. Why can't I feel good most days?

I have accepted my lot in life. I know to enjoy the good days. When they happen, I don't know when the next time will be. I so hope I feel this same way tomorrow. I want to feel good. I am a good person. I deserve to feel good. But deserving means nothing when it comes to bipolar disorder.

I see other people who feel good regularly. I see them getting things done. I see them laughing easily. I see them engaged in life. On a normal day, I don't feel any of those things. I do less. I don't laugh, and I don't feel engaged in life.

I have developed tools to make the best of my life. I make short to-do lists so I don't get stressed. I have my quiet time. I try to get the negative thoughts out of my brain. I do all this just to get by.

Today I feel good. I am doing things without thinking about it. I don't have to force it. I laugh. I don't have negative thoughts.

The realization brought on by feeling good, and that this is not normal for me, brings tears to my eyes. They won't last because I feel too good to dwell on tears.

At night, on a good day, I hope I have another good day tomorrow. But I don't know if I will. Usually my good days don't last.

So today I am going to be happy. I am going to get a lot done. I am going to feel good about this. I am going to nurture this happiness. I am going to remember this day. I am going to remember the good feeling I have today, and I am going to cherish it.

Comments

"Wow. I've written this exact same thing in my journal: 'I wonder who I'll wake up as tomorrow?' I hate the randomness of bipolar. I wake up depressed—why? No reason. I wake up happy—why? No reason. I've also written, 'I feel good today FOR NO REASON AT ALL.' I've come to realize that bipolar itself causes this. It isn't always because of a trigger. I've been stable for a while now, so I don't have to deal with this issue as much anymore. But I still get spooked when I feel really good for no apparent reason. It's sad that I have to second guess my emotions."

"Oh my gosh, the title alone made me feel understood. Then the article, well, that's me. Some days I do six loads of laundry, do the grocery shopping, go to the pharmacy, and swish out the toilets. Other days, I open a cabinet door with the intention of cleaning it out… one look overwhelms me, and I go back to the couch. There's the me that digs, weeds, and plants for two to three hours in the morning and the me that just wants the energy to turn on the sprinkler and remember to turn it off. I don't tell people. Friends know I've had depression and PTSD all my life, but they don't know that the term 'bipolar' was added a couple of years ago. I take three medications and do therapy and still struggle. But it would be far worse without those meds. So I try to be grateful for the good days, accepting of the no-motivation days, and forgiving of the irritable days."

"This article completely describes my life. Nice to read as it reminds me that I am not alone on this daily roller-coaster ride of highs and lows."

"Oh, yes, the 'how am I going to feel today or even tomorrow?' dilemma. Just thinking about it is strenuous and downright depressing. I see people on the streets, family, friends just being. Being happy, joking around, telling stories, etc. as I sit and ask myself, *Why don't I feel this way? Why can't I do the same?* Is it the bipolar? The depression that comes with it? Also for me, BPD? That uncertainty makes me feel a little scared, but I try because that's all I can do. I try, and I fail most times because all I end up doing is sleeping all day and not even eating a healthy meal. But...I continue to try."

3 | The Never-Ending To-Do List

For me, most days bloom with promise and hope. They end with more undone items on my never-ending to-do list.

~

Is your to-do list like mine? I make one out every day with the best intentions. I feel good when I do. It gives me a picture of what my day will look like. I know if I finish my list, I will be happy and satisfied.

My best intentions hardly ever translate into accomplishing the things on my list. Even though I keep it short and realistic, I never seem to get it all done.

Something happens. I have the hardest time getting started. Come *on*, I say to myself. *Get the first one done, and the rest will be easier.* But I put it off. I can't quite get going.

I know that my depression is actively sabotaging me. I know it. Somehow it takes my best intentions and throws them against the wall, breaking them into unmanageable pieces. So I sit. I think, *I will start at 10:00 a.m.* However, 10:00 a.m. comes, and I am still sitting.

Finally after an hour or two, I get up the energy to get to work on the first item. Slowly I work on it, and slowly I get it done. I put a load of laundry in the washing machine. I check it off my list. Then I sit down again to plan how to do the next item.

I am as motivated as I can be. It is just not enough. I try and try to get going on the second item, but my mind wanders. *I will get to it in a minute*, I say. Right after I check my e-mail. Then I check the news and read a few articles.

Finally I get back to my list. By now it is afternoon. My list says to do the dishes. This is a ten-minute job. I get up and start. Once I start, it is easy. I get the dishwasher loaded and the counters cleaned off. I pat myself on the back.

Now I go back to check it off my list, and I sit. I feel good for a while. I will just rest for a few minutes and move the laundry to the dryer. And again I sit. Things become even harder. My depression worsens. Oh, how I miss hypomania.

OK. *I can do it*, I decide. I get up and transfer the laundry. I pick up one of the garbage bags and carry it out. Again I sit down to cross it off the list.

It is Monday, and I am running out of time. I look at the list and skip three easy items. One is a phone call. This is the hardest of the three. I can't do it right now. I would have to talk to someone. The depression has a hold of me. Talking to someone right now is more than I can do.

By now it is late afternoon. I get up to take the laundry out of the dryer. I set it on the couch. All I have to do is fold it and take it upstairs and I am done with item number one. I take some deep breaths. All of a sudden this is an insurmountable task.

I want to check this off my list. I tell myself I can do it. I start to fold and stack. It is not a big load.

It has been a regular day. Six items on my to-do list. Three checked off. It is evening now. I can relax, and I do.

I start my list for tomorrow. It consists of today's items and a few new ones like take the laundry upstairs. Empty the dishwasher? I will do that in the morning.

Tomorrow's list becomes longer than today's. With the best intentions, I plan to get it done.

And now I sit. I am dissatisfied and out of energy. Today was a good day, I tell myself. I got some things done instead of fighting my demons *all* day. Tomorrow will be better.

For me, most days bloom with promise and hope. They end with more undone items on my never-ending to-do list. Some will get done. Some will fall off. But one thing is for sure. The list will never get done, and a pang of dissatisfaction and guilt stays with me day after day.

Comments

"Thank you for a well-written article that I desperately needed to read today. This is me. The depression side of bipolar two is so overwhelming and so hard to explain to my loved ones. The guilt of not doing my part rips me up inside. My list gets longer and more difficult to accomplish. One month, then six months go by. Where have I been? Sitting on the couch with my unfinished list. I am hopeful that a recent med adjustment will help. I have seen a ray of light this past week, if only for short periods of time. New psychiatrist and new therapist as well. I want to feel hope again."

"Love your posts, Dave. I, too, am an inveterate list maker. But that's all the further I get: making the list. I write down absolutely everything that could possibly ever need to be done ever, and then I get overwhelmed. That's when my depression really sits on my shoulder. I feel completely worthless for not having accomplished anything I set out to do. Not a single thing crossed off. And with my Swiss-cheese-like memory, I don't remember to do something if I don't write it down in at least three places. I have three calendars for appointments. (See any connection here? Threes. One of my obsessions.) My dining room table is covered with to-do reminders written on scraps of paper. Beside my chair is a clipboard with reams of notebook paper with lists of things to do, to throw away, to sell; people to write to, call, e-mail. My mom always said that once

I wrote it down, my brain considered it done, and I never get around to the physical act of actually doing something: as long as it's written down, it's done. But then the seeds I bought to plant in the spring are still in packets in September, the fabric I bought to make a garment is still in the bag months later, boxes of beautiful beads lay loose and not made into jewelry. Sigh. I'm so glad I'm not alone in List Land!"

"We must be the same person or at least related. I was shaking my head at everything you said. That is so me. I can't remember anything anymore. I've tried lists, calendars, entering them into my phone, you name it. Then I don't even remember to look at it."

4 | Suffering in Silence

As I hid in the shadows, doing all I could to just be there and not run away and escape, my anxiety would grow, and panic attacks were common. In my mind, I knew that all the people were staring at me and seeing my private thoughts of fear.

～

Most family get-togethers have been an exercise in hiding in the shadows and not wanting to be noticed. God forbid someone would come up to me and want to talk. I wouldn't look them in the eye because I knew if they looked in my eyes, they could see my soul and the pain, insecurity, embarrassment, and humiliation that were there.

A conversation with me would be me answering in one-word sentences. I would hope that the interaction would be as brief as possible, and I would do all I could to make that happen.

If I saw someone approaching, I would become the least interesting man in the world. I would be the last guy someone would want to have a conversation with.

As I hid in the shadows, doing all I could to just be there and not run away and escape, my anxiety would grow, and panic attacks were common. In my mind, I knew that all the people were staring at me and seeing my private thoughts of fear.

I had to escape. I had to. I began to look for my wife to tell her I had to go to the car. She was disappointed but understood. I looked for the most inconspicuous way to leave and slip out unnoticed.

Once out, I felt such relief. The car was my refuge. I could recline the seats and let the anxiety and panic slowly fade away. But it wasn't that easy. The pain and embarrassment and guilt hung on like sticky glue.

I felt guilt for having left my wife to answer the question, "Where's Dave?" The difference between being inside and out was only the proximity to the people. When someone came or went, I slipped lower in the seat. God forbid they saw me.

Hiding in the shadows was my life for decades. The fear of people seeing into my soul was constant. I took to wearing sunglasses because they hid my eyes. They gave me a sense of calmness. People couldn't see into my soul, I thought.

This weekend, we went to a barbeque. It was well attended. I talked to people I knew. I looked at them.

The embarrassment and pain were gone. However, strangers were a different experience.

I could feel that anxiety from the past. I still hid in the shadows and hoped no one talked to me. When they did, I still used one-word answers and ended the conversation as soon as possible.

My teaching stand-up comedy to folks with a mental illness made talking to people I knew easier. Telling them about my experiences teaching and performing and writing my book made me interesting, and I liked that response from people.

This weekend, I still watched the clock to see if it was time to leave—the earlier, the better. We left shortly after dinner, another escape.

One day I hope to stop hiding in the shadows. I hope to welcome conversations with new people. I hope to heal my soul so I can feel OK about people looking me in the eyes.

One day I hope to just heal. I don't know if this day will ever come. This is one more pain of living with bipolar disorder.

And those of you with bipolar disorder who go to these family picnics and other events, you are very brave. Pat yourself on the back for facing your fear and suffering in silence. Sometimes it is better to hide in public than to hide alone.

Comments

"Thank you so much for this article! I, too, have severe anxiety and bipolar. Your story of hiding in the shadows is me exactly! I am recently diagnosed, so it is somewhat comforting to read stories like this to know you're not alone. Day by day!"

"WOW, did you hit the nail on the head! I have to attend many of my husband's work-related parties and still have to force myself to engage in conversation. I still want to hide in a corner. I feel like I have 'BP' written on my forehead. He has a new job, so I'm trying to think of it as a new start but have already gone to one and still second guessing everything I said to everyone (three people) that I talked to. I'm so afraid of looking like a fool and saying something stupid. We are in a new city where I know NO ONE. These get-togethers are excruciating."

"How true! For years, I hide from just about everyone. The closet in my room was my only comfort zone. Then I took a number of writing courses and started to express how I felt on paper. I wrote a book and started talking about it. I still have occasions when many people are present that I have to leave because of panic attacks, but I am now speaking publicly to get the word out about stigma still being alive and well. I've come a long way, but I still have a long way to go!"

"I do this constantly, and it breaks my heart. I want to run and hide because I'm so embarrassed. Then I might babble on a second time about it if someone sees my cast, and the same thing will happen. I can see it in their eyes that sometimes they stay because they are so polite, but they want to escape, and then they get away from me at the first possible moment. I end up being a pariah at the social gathering rather quickly, and I retreat into a corner with tears in my eyes."

5 | Bipolar Disorder and Job Insecurity

I have lost many jobs due to my illness for both actions I took while manic and the inaction of depression.

~

For every working person with bipolar disorder, job insecurity is a constant concern. The question is, "Will my bipolar symptoms cause me to lose my job?"

My experience is that we want to work. We want independence and the ability to support ourselves and our families. We want the satisfaction that work provides, and we want the respect that comes with having a living-wage job.

We are vulnerable though. Even on the best medications, our bipolar disorder brings with it ups and downs. During the ups, we take risks that aren't necessarily good for our employers. We may be flippant and overly confident.

When we are depressed, our energy is sapped from us. Anxiety and the realization that we are not doing our job as well as we should make us feel vulnerable. We try and try to do our best, but at times our illness holds us back. In depression, no amount of cheerleading, self-help books, or inspirational sticky notes on our bathroom mirror can overcome the power of the illness.

Both mania and depression threaten our employment. When this happens, we know we are vulnerable to job loss. For too many of us, this vulnerability comes to fruition by being let go, laid off, or downsized. Whatever the terminology, the result is the same.

When this happens, we search for work as best as we can. However, the impact on our lives of being unemployed creates self-doubt and strains our relationships. Husbands, wives, fathers, and mothers, we struggle with the reality of a changing lifestyle.

So much of our self-worth is connected to working and supporting our families and ourselves. For many of us, our depression makes it incredibly challenging to get another job. We can't project self-confidence.

At interviews, we are flat. No matter how good our résumés, inside we believe we don't deserve the job, and if we get the job, we know we can't perform at the level necessary to be successful. We believe that if we get the job, inevitably we will get let go again.

Too often, people we love leave us. Our depression deepens. Our identities as a husband or wife, mother or father are shattered. We are lost and drifting. We lose our home. Friends disappear. We end up alone with our loss and the failure we feel.

How can we avoid this reality? Instead of suffering in silence, we have to talk about it with the people we love and with our therapist or family doctor. Expressing our fears helps us face them. Sharing the burden makes it more bearable.

I have lost many jobs due to my illness for both actions I took while manic and the inaction of depression. With the strength and support of my wife, counseling, and medications, we have been able to rebuild our lives.

Today, I know I can't work full time, so I work part time. I know too much stress triggers anxiety and depression, so I do low-stress work. I have adjusted my lifestyle to this reality. This adjustment was very difficult, and it took years to be OK with the changes.

As people with bipolar disorder, we have an inner strength that comes from living with so many challenges. Because of this inner strength, we persevere.

Job insecurity is part of our world. It is a burden we carry. But we don't have to carry this burden alone. Share it here as a comment for others to read. This will reduce the burden and help people in our bphope community know they are not alone. Share your story and make a difference.

Comments

"Well, it happened again. This time the reason was 'job elimination.'"

"Thank you, Dave. Now I know this is not just me and my life. You put into words all the thoughts that I never verbalized, or if I try to talk about it, even my son just thinks I am a loser."

"I've been fired from every job I've had except the last, when I resigned because I became severely out of whack, and working was one of my biggest triggers. It's been seven years now since I've worked, and I don't think I could return to my previous line of work (veterinary technician). My skills are outdated, and I don't have any other workplace skills. The inability to work has made me feel like a huge burden. When times are tough with money, it's hard not to beat myself up, knowing everything would be better if I just got a job like a 'normal person.'"

"For me, it's always a case of taking work 'below my level.' I, too, have had to accept that working full time is bad for me. As much as I'd like to do something more fulfilling, I carry all the fears expressed here that one day, it will all go wrong."

6 | Too Depressed to Shower

I read a newspaper article a couple of months ago that said people are showering way too often.

◡

Today I am going to talk about bipolar disorder being good for the environment. Who knew? I read a news story a couple months ago that people are showering way too often. The story said that we only need to shower once a week; and more than that and we are wasting water and washing off essential oils that are good for us. I thought, *With bipolar depression, I am way ahead of this trend.*

Think of what I am saving in shampoo and soap not going down the sewers. I mean, I am good for the environment. And then there is laundry. When I have bipolar depression, I am not doing laundry. I'm lucky if I change my clothes. And sometimes I sleep in my clothes so I don't have to take them off and put them back on. So I am not using phosphates; I am saving water, electricity, and gas. Heck, I'm saving the environment.

And I'm thinking that when I am depressed, I don't drive anywhere, so I save gas and emissions. At this point, I am really good for the environment.

So when I disappear in my depression, and someone says, "Where have you been?" I say, "I have been taking care of the environment." And when they ask what I have been doing, I say I have just been very environmentally conscious. Who knew?

So I think I am going to enter a contest for the most environmentally friendly person in the world. I think I will win because who else is going to admit that they only take a shower every other week? Good idea, huh? So thanks for listening. I appreciate it. Tongue in cheek.

Comments

"Great article, Dave. Also, I've read quite a few of the comments. It's great to know I'm not alone and also that I'm saving the environment; just as well, given I'm pro-environment."

"I've been piling up laundry for about a month. I won't be doing it 'til next year, ha-ha. I wait until I have no clean underwear to wear."

"Hmmmm…I hadn't looked at it that way before! Also good for the economy as we just purchase new socks and underwear when our clean underthings store wanes. So much easier to buy new than to do laundry and thus harm the environment. Thanks!"

"Oh my goodness, this had me literally howling out so loud my neighbors probably think I'm losing my mind. Oh, wait, I'm ahead of the curve on that! WOW. Thanks so much for the gift of laughter you've given me tonight. I really needed it. I'm still smiling so much as I write this that my face is starting to hurt. I think I'll read it over again so I can be in stitches one more time before I go to bed. Thanks, Dave!"

"Omgosh. I read this as I lay in bed past noon, in my clothes that I haven't gotten out of in over a week. I say I love you, Dave Mowry! Trying to have humor here! I'm bipolar green."

7 | Panic Attacks

After a panic attack, it takes days to recover. The anxiety lingers, and I feel weak. The self-loathing doesn't go quietly. I am fragile and alone.

～

*M*y bipolar panic attacks are short lived but crippling. In the middle of one, I feel fear, anxiety, and helplessness. My heart pounds, my breathing goes shallow, and sweat builds on my forehead, back, and armpits, soon to soak my shirt. My self-image plummets.

While this is happening, I know people are staring at me. I know they are judging me. I know they are saying, "That guy's a loser."

After a panic attack, it takes days to recover. The anxiety lingers, and I feel weak. The self-loathing doesn't go quietly. I am fragile and alone.

I know many of you share these experiences. For some of you, the panic attacks are in the past. You have managed your way through them, and they are now just bad memories.

For me, they are still present yet milder. I call them mini panic attacks. When I start to go on my downward spiral, I catch it early and am able to calm myself—not all the way but enough that the full-blown attacks are mostly in the past.

And that is one thing I want to say. It can get better. Some days I would have three or four attacks. Today they are rare. My mind has recovered over time. The pain is not so raw. I lose control of my brain less often.

Everyone with bipolar disorder has panic attack stories. Here are some of mine.

Of all places, one would not think of getting a haircut as panic inducing. But for me it was. First, it takes lots of energy to get out of the house. My self-worth is already low. Somehow I dodge the neighbors so I don't have to talk to them. Talking to them triggers a panic attack.

I just want my hair cut. I don't want to talk to this stranger. I don't want to lie to them. I don't dare tell them the truth. And they always want to talk. I answer with one-word responses and say as little as possible, hoping they get the hint. And if they continue to want a two-way conversation, I start to sweat, first on my forehead and then the top of my head and the back of my neck.

Once the sweat started, it was like opening the flood gates. Anxiety leads to sweat, and sweat leads to more anxiety and panic. I want to escape. But I sit there and die for another ten minutes before I am done. It was embarrassing and humiliating. I dreaded getting a haircut, and every time it took great energy to go and get one.

Some other places where I had panic attacks may be familiar. For one who has not experienced it, this won't make sense. I know. It doesn't make sense to me. It was just my own private little hell.

I would have a panic attack in school when I had to participate in small groups because I couldn't hide.

I would have a panic attack waiting to introduce myself to a group. As it got closer to my turn, I panicked more and more. God forbid I had to say something.

One of the worst experiences was running into an old acquaintance. I would immediately go into panic mode and have to escape as soon as possible.

At back-to-school night with my kids, I knew that everyone was looking at me. I knew they could see my soul and my panic. There is nothing worse than melting down in front of your kids.

How about one of my favorites, seeing a neighbor on the way to the mailbox? It is brief, so the panic from the interaction occurs on the way back from the mailbox.

Then there is hearing a knock at the door. Oh my God, can't I hide?

I could go on, but you know the story. Each attack took a little more out of me and made me more prone to the next.

Today, things are better for me. I still want to hide a lot, but it is not the overwhelming need to escape.

Writing this helps. Thanks for reading.

Dave Mowry

Comments

"Thank you for sharing this. I suffer from panic attacks and anxiety. So many of the situations you mentioned ring true for me. Answering the phone is also a biggie. I am working on ways to cope, but the mindfulness and meditation approaches don't seem to be helping. I am working on medication trials to find something but am frustrated."

"I've recently found this site, and in a way, I don't feel so alone…"

"Over the last month, I've been suffering from crippling anxiety and depression. I find myself unable to barely get out of bed. The thought of leaving the house can bring me to tears. I feel so empty and broken. I've felt with bipolar the last seventeen years (I'm now thirty-five). I just want to say thank you."

8 | Don't Disappear from My Life because I Have Bipolar Disorder

I got pretty good at predicting when relationships would end: first the sympathy, then the "got to go," and finally the unconvincing excuses for not seeing each other.

⁓

When I was first diagnosed with bipolar disorder, I had friends, relationships, and business contacts. I thought, *These people know me. I can tell them that I have bipolar disorder, and our relationships will continue.* Boy, was I wrong.

As I told people, one at a time they would start dropping out of my life. There were the unreturned phone calls. There were the invitations that stopped coming or weren't followed up on. There were the no-shows.

Seeing someone on the street was awkward. I would greet them, and they were always in a hurry to move along. Then there were the ones who saw me coming and ignored me altogether.

All of these experiences made me feel like less of a person than I was before. My circle of friends and acquaintances shrank considerably. There was the being treated differently. The question "How are you doing?" had a touch of sympathy and sadness to it. I wasn't dying, folks. But I felt it in them.

I got pretty good at predicting when relationships would end: first the sympathy, then the "got to go," and finally the unconvincing excuses for not seeing each other.

Then on a larger scale there was no invitation to the high school reunion because Dave has bipolar disorder. "Oh, that's so sad. He was such a good guy," they would say. No invitation to Phil's barbeque/birthday party. "Where is Dave?" someone would ask. "Oh, haven't you heard? Dave is bipolar."

The invites to the Super Bowl party that didn't come were hard. I rationalized that it was more fun to watch the game in peace and quiet. But it wasn't really. I rationalized a lot.

Last week I thought about this, and I turned it around. What did these folks miss by not having me there?

They missed my friendly smile and my sincere and curious questions of what was happening with them. They missed my humor. They missed my compassion and enthusiasm for life.

They missed seeing that someone with bipolar disorder is just a regular guy with hopes and dreams.

They missed my amazing and inspirational recovery. They missed hearing about me writing my book *No, Really, We Want You to Laugh*, and at the end of the process, they missed getting a free signed copy.

They missed my transition to teaching stand-up comedy to folks with a mental illness and performing.

They missed the interesting, caring, passionate, and motivational person I have become, who just happens to have bipolar disorder.

Today I have new friends and relationships. I am liked and respected. I share myself fully. I am a good person and a good friend.

Do I reach back? Why? For most, the answer is no. For some, the answer is maybe. It is scary. People may still reject me.

Is a relationship that ended in hurt and ignorance worth rebuilding? I will let you know when I find out.

But today I am at peace. I think I will stay here for a little while longer.

Comments

"Congratulations!! You are awesome. Good for you! So happy that you found yourself and found a cozy place to fit in. I, too, suffered loss of friendships, being part of a group. Even was rejected by some at my church. It was excruciating because rejection, especially by women, was always a sore spot for me. I even lost my job in nursing twice with two huge NYC hospices because of my diagnosis but can't prove discrimination. It all but killed me. But I, too, have risen up in other ways. Or at least fighting to come back. We have to. We are the same people, and it does recede. The more understanding, support, and love, the better we are. I'm very happy for you."

"Wow. I experienced the mass exodus of what I felt were close friends. At seventeen, I had never experienced the adversity that most in life experience at some time. Apart from my mental illness onset and subsequent hospitalizations, everything had and has been rather normal. After experiencing acute mental illness, my close friends stuck by me (at a distance) for a year or two max. Now I am able to relate closely to my adult literacy students who have complicated yet fulfilling and valuable lives. I am using my abilities to help them earn their GEDs and improve themselves. I will never forget how difficult it was for me to be excluded from the society I was previous part of and how difficult it is for me to grasp the limits my former friends and some family members have in relating to the individuals in our society as a whole. Mental illness is hell, but when I was thirty-seven, I finally reentered society in a way I would have never been able to without having gone through (and continuing to go through) what I have."

"It is so true. I once had a sizable number of friends, but since the onset of my illness, I have watched them all desert me—people I had previously gone out of my way for. I'm beginning to come to terms with the fact that they were never truly my friends."

9 | Flashbacks

Is this a curse I have to live with, constantly vulnerable to what seems to be whims of my mind? Will I ever get away from the dark days of my past? Will I ever get away from loss, pain, fear, anxiety, and embarrassment? How many times do I have to relive an experience before I can move on?

～

For the past few years, it seemed as though my triggers and constant flashbacks from my bipolar disorder were under control. I started thinking about my experiences differently. A negative thought would pass without the pain of reliving the experience.

But last week the triggers and flashbacks came back with a vengeance. I have no idea why. My anxiety increased, and although deep breathing helped, I still went back to the hard experiences and memories. I felt the embarrassment, fear, anxiety, and loss like my experience was yesterday.

Today is better. But I am wondering if I am going back to those dark days. I can't. I won't.

Reliving the pain of people disappearing from my life, reliving mistakes I have made, reliving loss of myself through my insanity—these painful memories and the guilt, anxiety, and fear they bring back is no way to live.

I get triggered by a song or a thought or any reminder about just about anything having to do with the impact of my bipolar disorder. The stress and anxiety build in my chest. The feelings of guilt and self-doubt add another layer. And then pain, embarrassment, and a sense of dread come in a wave on top of that.

These painful feelings can last from a minute to hours. When they last for more than a few minutes, the residual feeling can last days. My confidence drops, and my thoughts return again and again to my dark days.

I learned to control these experiences about five years ago by learning stand-up comedy. I looked for the humor in my experiences and wrote jokes about my life with mental illness. I learned through a program called Stand Up for Mental Health.

I didn't make fun of myself. I looked for and found the humor in some of my darkest days. It changed the way I think. Instead of having an anxiety attack from a memory triggered by a song, I would think about how I could find the humor in it and then write a joke about it. Doing this gave me control over my experiences instead of my experiences having control over me. Now I teach stand-up comedy to other folks with mental illness and see the same transformation happen to them.

I wrote a book about the impact that comedy had on other people. The book is called *No, Really, We Want You to Laugh*. It tells the story of six "comics" whose lives were changed. By looking for the humor in our hard experiences, we create new pathways in our brains. With continued use, these pathways become stronger. The old negative ones become weaker, and we are able to move on.

But last week the thoughts and anxiety broke through again. I know this happens to others with bipolar disorder because I hear their stories as a certified peer support specialist and stand-up comedy teacher.

Now I wonder why this happens. I have looked at all the usual factors: sleep, diet, exercise. For me there was no reason that I can find. These negative thoughts came out of nowhere.

Is this a curse I have to live with, constantly vulnerable to what seems to be whims of my mind? Will I ever get away from the dark days of my past? Will I ever get away from loss, pain, fear, anxiety, and embarrassment? How many times do I have to relive an experience before I can move on?

And yet I have hope. I have had years of freedom from these triggers and flashbacks. Today I am going to look at my demons, and I am going to try to find the humor in them. Today I am going to write jokes about them. Today I am going to start having control over them again instead of them having control over me.

Therefore it seems appropriate that I leave you with one of my favorite jokes I have written and tell on stage.

I think there should be a dating service for folks with a mental illness. I can see the postings now: "paranoid white male seeks paranoid white female to share compound in Idaho." Or "paranoid female seeks male with no government connections." Or, my favorite, "dual personality female seeks dual personality male... for double dates."

Enjoy sharing this with others because *No, Really, I Want You to Laugh*.

Comments

"Oh my God, YES, you described what I've been trying to put words to! Flashbacks. I have these ALL. THE. TIME. and the horrible physical sensations that come along with them. They happen randomly all day long every single day, and I don't know how to stop them, and meds don't seem to have any influence."

"Thank you. It is with tears in my eyes that I write this. I am fifty-eight years old, and I have NEVER heard anyone describe what I go through so well. At one time I was diagnosis with bipolar...don't think anyone knows...my diagnosis now is clinical reoccurring depression and anxiety...one thing: instead of getting anxiety, I cry. The grief is unbearable at times. Thank you for sharing."

"I have flashbacks most days, throughout the day. They are short (a minute or less) but very painful. One thing I try is to have a word or short phrase that I say to help myself snap out of it. Also when I think about the past, I try to imagine what I would say/do if another person was doing/feeling the content of the flashback. Usually I find that my judgment of the person I was at that time in the past is much harsher and more negative than judgments I make about other people. So now sometimes I think, *That poor girl* or reflect on the context of my behavior."

"Thank you so much for these thoughts. They hit home. I, too, have continued to lapse into those moments of losing great friends, guilt in my behaviors, embarrassment, low self-esteem from inner thoughts that continually run through my head, isolation, and fear of not trusting myself. I am blessed with family that understands—even though they have paid the price for all my bipolar episodes over the years. Thank God for compassion, love, and forgiveness. My daughter sent me this link because I am once again in the process of dread and the lack of movement forward in my life: it seems just as I am moving and stretching to a more positive path, it hits. This article says so much of what I feel and have a hard time expressing. I am sad for all the things I've desired to do in my life—yet I have yet found a way to move forward. Being sixty-one, there is an urgency to change to expand and live my life in these final years. Regrets, yes. Loneliness, yes. Feeling sorry for myself, no. Progress, yes. Desire to somehow take control, yes. Drive, yes. Grief, yes: for my life changing forever at forty (cognitive damage after many rounds of chemo for ovarian and breast cancer—neither of which did I ever ask, "Why me?" about). I have always loved life and never avoided its many challenges, yet now I don't feel in control and feel I lost so much of my young life. The ups and downs have taken their toll. This is good—it has allowed me to express so much of what I feel. I am grateful for your story and openness."

10 | Is Laughter Really the Best Medicine?

During my conversation with Julie, I remembered the first time I laughed out loud after years of suffering with my bipolar depression and anxiety. It was 2011, and I can remember the laugh as if it were yesterday. It was my first belly laugh in fifteen years.

~~

This week I was talking to Julie Fast, columnist for *bp Magazine for Bipolar* at bphope.com (Fast Talk). You can read more about Julie at therealjuliefast.com. She is a bestselling author and a regular blogger at bphope.com/blog.

We were talking about the therapeutic value of laughter. This was natural because I teach stand-up comedy classes through Stand Up for Mental Health in Oregon, standupformentalhealth.com, to other folks with a mental illness. Then we do shows that help break stigma one joke at a time.

Laughter has been shown to have psychosocial and social benefits. And therapeutic laughter is mainly derived from spontaneous laughter. Studies suggest that there is sufficient evidence to suggest that laughter has positive effects on mental illness—so much so that it would be appropriate for laughter to be used as a complementary/alternative medicine in the prevention and treatment of illness.

During my conversation with Julie, I remembered the first time I laughed out loud after years of suffering with my bipolar depression and anxiety. It was 2011, and I can remember the laugh as if it were yesterday. It was my first belly laugh in fifteen years.

That one laugh triggered a feeling of peace and normalcy that I had not felt in such a long time. It was fleeting at first. But it was a break from the constant feeling of sadness, depression, and worthlessness that was my life.

Can laughter do for others what it does for me? By teaching comedy, I can share that feeling with others. I can share the joy with others. I see the change in others.

One can't feel anxious, angry, or sad while laughing. It reduces stress and allows you to see things in a realistic and nonthreatening way. Humor strengthens relationships, too, by triggering positive feelings and emotional connectedness. When we laugh with one another, a positive bond is created.

Abe Lincoln recognized the value of laughter. He said, "Gentlemen, why don't you laugh? With the fearful strain that is upon me day and night, if I did not laugh I should die, and you need this medicine as much as I do."

Besides talking about the value of laughter in our lives, my goal today is to make you laugh. I have a joke that I tell from the stage when I have a show.

When I went into the psych unit, I was confused. I thought it was a hotel. On the second day, I met with a psychiatrist, and he asked me how it was going. I said, "Not too bad, but the service here sucks. I ordered a margarita when I got here, and it still hasn't arrived yet." He said, "Oh" and wrote something down on his pad. Then he asked if I knew where I was. And I said, "Well, my wife said it was going to be a surprise. I'm hoping St. Thomas." "No," he said, "it's St. Elsewhere." I said, "Oh, is that in the Caribbean?"

The impact of writing and telling these jokes has been amazing for me. When people hear me joke about my mental illness, they see me as a regular person with a sense of humor. They laugh with me. They no longer look at me with pity or whisper when I am around. I no longer suffer in silence.

My next post on May 25 is going to provide tools to find humor in our experiences. While some of these experiences are too raw, others are ripe for humor. I hope to help you see the difference and find the funny where there is sadness and regret. The title of the next blog is going to be "No, Really, I Want You to Laugh." I can't wait to share this amazing tool that changed my life.

Comments

"My father was a famous gag writer and never serious. Comedy was his way of coping. BP? But a father who is never serious is entertaining but frustrates his kids. I don't laugh often though I like acting in comic amateur dramatics. In Belgium, there are laughter clubs, though I haven't joined one yet."

11 | Having Bipolar and Finding Your Funny

Finding humor in my dark days has changed my life. So how do we get past the pain even for a few hours?

~

*H*aving a mental illness and being in the depths of depression or the highs of mania is not funny. But some of the things we do during these experiences can be ripe for humor—if we can get past the pain.

Finding humor in my dark days has changed my life. So how do we get past the pain even for a few hours?

I believe our brain pathways have been developed to take us to the feelings of guilt, embarrassment, and pain over years and years. By thinking in a different way, we can change those pathways.

Let's start with depression. The beginning of finding our funny is to just stay with the feeling depression brings. Breathe deep. Just let yourself feel it. That's your old pathway. Our thoughts lead to feelings. That's how our brains and bodies work.

But we can change our thoughts when we are not in the grasp of our illness. We can change how we think.

To change that thought process, state the obvious: "I was/am terribly depressed." Now for the different thought. Say to yourself, "So how depressed am I?" Now go for the less obvious. "I am so depressed…" Now think of something not obvious. How about, "I'm so depressed I sleep under my mattress"?

Let's try discrimination. "I have been discriminated against." State the obvious. "People treat me differently when they find out I have bipolar disorder." Now state the not so obvious. "As someone with a mental illness, I see discrimination where others don't. Take happy hour, for instance. I think that is being discriminatory. There should also be a crappy hour for depressed people. And people with bipolar disorder could go to both."

So where do you see discrimination? At work? At school? With family? Now think of the unexpected. How about the bathtub? Or the local restaurant? Let's take the restaurant. What would be a menu item that is discriminatory? Scrambled eggs? Take your time. Let your mind wander. Relax. Breathe. Remember, your brain is developing a new pathway. It is developing a new way of thinking about things.

Probably nothing funny will come to mind right now. But spend a little time with it. Google "weird breakfasts." Today or maybe tomorrow you will think of something. Humor doesn't have to be real. Make up a breakfast item—like two eggs over depressed.

When you do think of something funny, you will smile, and it will feel good. Your brain will want to go there again. And in the future when you think of discrimination, your mind will go to the breakfast and not to the negative feelings from before.

Now do it again with an experience you had while manic that was embarrassing. Feel the embarrassment. Stay with it. That's your pathway. Now think, *I was so embarrassed I…*now let your mind wander. What is the first thought that come to mind? Let that go. How about "I was so embarrassed I called my phone so I could hang up on myself"?

Now you have some info to find some funny in your hard experiences. As you change your pathways, you gain control over your experiences. You will probably even laugh for the first time in a long time.

Find a friend to share your funny with. The more you think it and say it, the stronger the pathways become.

In my book *No, Really, We Want You to Laugh*, my coauthor, Tara Rolstad, and I tell the stories of six people who found their funny in this way and how it changed their lives. You can find some funny in the hard times. Try it with an open mind. Your brain will like you for it.

Comments

"I was sitting in the ER during a particularly bad depressive episode, and the nurse was being quite patronizing. I turned to my companion and said, 'I'm crazy, not stupid.' He thought it was hysterical. I then proceeded to make up all kinds of ridiculous scenarios about hospitals for the mentally ill, like swimming pools with no water, but you still had to wear a life jacket and a golf course where you used swim noodles and balloons because balls and clubs are obviously too dangerous. It made a bad situation a little more bearable."

"I've long used this technique to get over episodes. It's easier to find humor in some episodes than others. It definitely helps to write. Thank you for your post."

12 | Five Surprising Things We Can Do to Improve Our Lives

And lastly, I do something a wise woman told me really helped her. It is something I never would have thought about by myself but makes a significant difference in my life…

～

I met a fellow last week at a NAMI (National Alliance on Mental Illness) meeting. He had a calm presence and a peaceful demeanor, and he was sincere and thoughtful. I wondered how he came to be so at peace with himself while living with bipolar disorder. I asked him, and here is what he told me. He said he does five things that I have never heard used together before.

He said, "Up until a few years ago, my life was one of anxiety, guilt, and unhappiness. I was stuck in my head with racing thoughts. Today I am happy. Even though I still have my ups and downs, my routine brings me back to calmness."

1. Be Kind

   "First, every day I try to do something nice for someone. This gets me out of my head as I think of someone else. Doing something nice can be as simple as sending an encouraging e-mail to someone. It can be as simple as holding the door open for someone or giving up my seat on the bus. The key for me is to keep it simple as I look for the opportunity to do something nice for someone else."

2. Enjoy the Simple Things

   "Another thing is that I do something nice for myself every day. I keep this simple too. Sometimes I take a nice, long shower. Sometimes I bake chocolate chip cookies from premade cookie dough and eat them with a glass of cold milk. This inevitably brings good feelings and good memories. Sometimes it is as simple as writing a few lines in my journal about something that went right recently. Looking to do something nice for myself every day gets me out of my head and helps me look forward to my day."

3. Create a To-Do List—and Tackle the Hardest Part First

   "As I look at my day or my week and see the things I need to do and want to do, I try to do the hardest thing first. I used to sit and stress about the hard things. I put them off, and in doing so I got stuck and full of anxiety. Then I would feel guilt for not doing them, and this created a road block, so I did not do the other, easier things on my list. Doing nothing made me feel like a failure. Doing the hardest thing on the list is just that: hard. It may be a phone call about a past-due bill. It may be paying bills or working on my taxes. Whatever it is, I do it first. That breaks the deadlock, and I am able to do the other things on the list. It improves my quality of life and gives me a sense of self-worth and confidence."

4. Take Time to Read

   "I also read for half an hour every day. I read something that is short and interesting or a book with short chapters that I can put down and pick up the next day and not lose my place. I have read Kay Redfield Jamison's *An Unquiet Mind.* And I enjoyed your book *No, Really, We Want You to Laugh.* When I read, it calms my mind. Doing this daily feels good and also accomplishes the goal of doing something nice for myself."

5. Watch the Cooking Channel

"And lastly, I do something a wise woman told me really helped her. It is something I never would have thought about by myself but makes a significant difference in my life. I watch the Cooking Channel every day. Watching the Cooking Channel is calming, educational, and surprisingly motivating. I relax without feeling like I am wasting my time. This gets me out of my head and gives me the energy to do other things like go to the grocery store for a few things or cook a simple dinner. Sometimes I cook a recipe from the show, which can also be found online at the Food Network website. But usually I create something with my newfound knowledge of what spices go best with chicken. Or I make mashed potatoes with some unique toppings. Afterward I get to enjoy a meal that I feel good about preparing. I find this is helpful and healthy for me.

"These are five things I try to do every day to improve my life. Each is not overwhelming, and all get me out of my head and away from my anxiety, guilt, and racing thoughts. Each helps me have calmness and peace of mind."

Comments

"This was amazing 4 me! It makes so much sense, yet I failed 2 realize such simple things can help so much! I also use the 'hard things first' method, and as hard as it is 2 do that, it makes my day/week feel smoother. Honestly, after that I'm lost (lol), but I can c how doing something nice 4 someone else would help. I find it hard 2 do nice things 4 myself whether depressed or manic as I don't feel worth the effort, but sometimes u just have 2 make yourself do it. We all know this struggle isn't easy, so any little thing that helps…"

"I didn't realize it until reading this article, but some of these are things I already do (well, except the Cooking Channel—I don't have cable)…I've 'practiced kindness' for a long time now because I know that putting goodness into the world helps me feel better too. I read short articles and stories several times per day. I try to find pleasure in simple things such as crafting and cooking—instead of the Cooking Channel, I use Pinterest to find new recipes. I've found some excellent recipes this way! My struggle comes with the to-do list. I still have a cycle of making one and putting things off until 'later.' Later I feel too tired or find something else I'd rather do…I'm definitely working on that."

"I have to tell you that I relate so well to your articles. When I read them, I think, *OH MY GOODNESS! I sooo get this*."

"I love the simplicity of the five tasks because my brain sometimes has trouble focusing for too long. It's like it's given me permission to keep it simple (in Australia, we would add 'stupid' to the end of that statement and still reap the benefits)."

13 | What Might Have Been

I had the same experience with friends. I made friends when I was level and lost them when I was depressed. I was lonely and sad. What might have been were solid relationships and feelings of inclusion.

⁓

As a person with bipolar disorder, I can't help but look back and think of what might have been. What would my life have been like if I did not have this mental illness? When I do this, I feel sadness and a sense of loss.

From about the age of twelve on, I remember the depression and anxiety. Both were overwhelming. But I also remember the good times. Those are the times when my illness was in remission and I was a high-functioning individual. However, the good times were always outweighed by the bad.

In my mid-twenties, I got a really good job at a well-respected company. Being well, I worked my way up to become a regional sales manager. I was successful and was highly paid. I wanted to continue my career there, and I was happy.

Then my mania got in the way. I began to feel invincible. I began to have unrealistic expectations. As my mania continued, I got more and more out of touch. This behavior was obvious to upper management even though I could not see it.

Soon I fell into depression as I always did after a manic episode. I became withdrawn and started to do my job poorly. Soon I was laid off, a polite term for being let go. What might have been were continued success and happiness. What I got were setback and loss.

This pattern continued. A year after I was laid off, I started my own company. Again the mania brought on unrealistic expectations and feelings of invincibility. Depression soon followed, and I had to get out. I just had to escape. I sold out for practically nothing.

The company went on to be a great success. The concept was sound, and the foundation was solid. Due to my bipolar disorder, I wasn't a part of that success. What might have been were success and financial independence.

It took years to recover from this experience. Eventually I leveled out and could participate in life again. I bought a Subway sandwich shop and grew to owning six. I had financial independence and a solid feeling of success.

In a few years, my bipolar came back with a vengeance. I ended up in the hospital to find relief from my overwhelming and debilitating anxiety and depression. I lost my business and our house. I lost it all. What might have been were independence, happiness, and success.

I had the same experience with friends. I made friends when I was level and lost them when I was depressed. I was lonely and sad. What might have been were solid relationships and feelings of inclusion.

My family life suffered also. And this is the most emotionally difficult. When I was stable, I had great relationships with my wife and kids. When the mania and depression came, I became isolated and detached. The anxiety and sadness overwhelmed me. I was less present for my family. I refer to this time as my lost years.

What might have been was a full family life of happiness and meaning. There would have been continuity and security instead of two years of homelessness. There would have been kids who brought friends around, kids who I didn't embarrass, and kids who, during that time, were proud of me.

Put these all together, and I have a lifetime of what might have been. I could have had stability instead of homelessness and financial success and security instead of losing it all. And most importantly, I could have had satisfaction and pride.

Some days I drift back and feel the sadness, the loss, and the failure. I will never really know what might have been. But I know I would have been whole.

Today I am mostly stable. I have good relationships with my wife and kids. I can write about my experiences, and people can relate and know they are not alone.

But I will never get over what might have been. Over time, I think of it less. But it will always be with me.

Comments

"I completely relate to this article. Recently I have been told that my bipolar might be 'cured' with the new dosage of medication I'm taking. Not only am I suspicious, but I cannot forget how my whole life has been altered up to this point by my bipolar experiences. How can I ever trust my brain again?"

"When I hook up with old friends or even when I think my future will be as bad as my past, I tell myself that I was sick. I was sick for twenty years, just like a person who has suffered from cancer or another illness or like a person who has gone to jail. Twenty years I lost. Twenty years I will never get back, and I will be lucky for twenty more. This is a horrible, horrific disorder."

"I understand your wondering about what might have been. I was not diagnosed until I was sixty-two. I find myself envying people who are diagnosed at a young age. I wonder what turn my life would have taken if I had had treatment as a teen or in my twenties. I try to only look at what will be, but my mind can't help going to what might have been."

"I always forget that I am not the only one who feels this way. I have been on antidepressants from the age of nineteen. Finally at about thirty, I got diagnosed with bipolar disorder. In the meantime, I lost two good jobs stemmed from going on disability. Things just went downhill from there. As of now I am thirty-eight, recently divorced, foreclosed house, and living with parents. I do have a part-time job that I like, but I see no way out. I look back at all the decisions I made and have such regret now that I see things better. I feel like I never got to experience my twenties, and it makes me so sad. It sounds dumb, but I watch TV shows and think, *I will never be able to do that.* Regret is an evil I cannot shake."

"My goodness, you are not alone! Are we related?! Ha! I have been through the exact same situation you have. Had been in a six-figure-paying job at twenty-three, owned my own house, great friends and family, a solid relationship, working out, and then BOOM—lost it all! Foreclosure and everything. My little sister no longer speaks to me. I'm on disability and get paid generously, but my father so badly wants me back in the corporate world. I can't. I cannot keep a job to save my life. I'm thirty-six and living with my parents and have no one and nothing. I even lost my beloved pets. I also might add that I went through mania so bad that I ended up incarcerated for six months. So trust me when I say you are not alone. I look at everyone and wish to God I had their lives no matter how bad they may be. They can't be any worse than mine! Hang in there!"

14 | Suicide Ideation

The suicide ideation I am talking about is not something we decide to think about. The reality is that the thoughts seem to wander into our minds—mostly when we are depressed...we wonder where they come from, but we never get to know.

(On a special note, my father committed suicide. His suicide took away some of the taboo. When I thought of ending my life, his decision somehow made it an easier decision for me.)

⁓

Talking about suicide ideation is taboo. However, for folks with bipolar disorder, it is real. Not talking about it doesn't change that.

Some think that talking about suicide makes it more likely that someone will follow through. That is not the case. Talking about it brings it into the open, where it can be talked about with family, friends, peers, therapists, and doctors.

The suicide ideation I am talking about is not something we decide to think about. The reality is that the thoughts seem to wander into our minds—mostly when we are depressed. But they wander in at other times too. We wonder where they come from, but we never get to know.

During my bouts of depression, thoughts of suicide pop into my head from time to time. I know I am not going to do it, but the thoughts stay around anyway.

During a recent class I was in, the subject came up. Everyone in the group has occasional thoughts of suicide. As we talked about it, I realized we all had stories to tell.

Everyone had their own recurring thoughts. *If I was going to commit suicide, how would I do it?* Staging accidents was the most popular. Running off the road into a tree is the thought that most often occurs to me.

Me? I have a tree picked out that would be perfect. It is on a windy road, which makes it so someone wouldn't see me run off the road on purpose. But it is not secluded, so I would be found right away.

It would look like an accident, so my life insurance would still pay off. People I care about would think it was an accident and so would not carry around the stigma of suicide.

There is also a curve on an old highway in the Columbia River Gorge where I could drive off a cliff. The drawback is that I may not be found for weeks.

I decided that jumping off a bridge is not for me. Drowning is a miserable way to go. And self-harm by weapon would leave too much weight on my family.

Pills are a possibility. But then again it would not look like an accident, and I wouldn't want to be in a situation where I have committed to the act, and then, as I am dying, I have second thoughts and feelings of guilt and panic. That to me is the worst possible thing that could happen, along with subjecting my family to guilt, shame, and blame.

Some people without bipolar disorder are going to read this and be horrified. That is why the topic is taboo. But it is a topic that can be discussed. Suicide ideation is a fact of life for those of us with bipolar disorder. Having it out in the open and talking about it with a loved one is a huge relief.

It is a huge relief to know we are not alone. It is a huge relief to know that others think about it and that in reality we would never follow through.

So the thoughts wander into our minds from time to time. We spend time with these thoughts. We think of ways to do it. We think of the details. We envision our funerals. But if the thoughts become too real, we stop. We put it out of our minds, knowing we will never do it and wondering why we think about it.

The thoughts fade, and our lives move forward. We appreciate life more and hold our friends and family closer.

Suicide ideation will come again. It is like an acquaintance that stops by occasionally. We spend time with it. We think about the hows and whys. And then the thoughts go away...until the next time.

If you or someone you know is thinking about suicide, get help now. The national suicide lifeline is: 1-800-273-8255.

Comments

"Wow. I sometimes have them every day. I have had a timeline since middle school, where I would postpone it to graduate high school, then college, then babies—always trying to figure out when a good time is. I thought when my youngest left for college would be the end because I thought I would be nothing not being a mother. I have postponed it again because not only do I see a future for my boys; I see one for myself. I am sure I will think about it. I have many medical issues, yet none are terminal—my luck. I know I don't want to be old and sickly. For now I have a lot to look forward to."

"I live with the thoughts. At one point they were a daily occurrence. Since I have met my partner, they are less prevalent, but they do come and bite me now and then. I guess I am a pessimistic optimist and always manage to hold them at bay...well, most times. I have attempted suicide five times but unsuccessfully. I figure in my most lucid moments that things will change if I'm still around, but to kill myself at a time when life is unbearable would only condemn me to an eternity of the same. The Samaritans have given me a safe place to discuss my thoughts and feelings about suicide and find my own truth and my path out of it. They have saved me so many times. It is good to talk and share."

"I hadn't heard of anyone else having a timeline. I always have. The ceiling rose as I grew older. I'm two years away from the last 'ceiling,' but I sort of want to go now, but there is always something getting in the way. This time it is my son's finals; I can't do anything to jeopardize that. Actually two years' time does seem an appropriate time as both my children will have finished their studies. If it comes down to it, I don't believe I can actually accomplish it no matter how many times I think about it."

"Wow. I thought I was the only one. If I miss my meds (which I do sometimes when I think I'm cured), I go straight to thinking suicide. It's like I have no middle ground—either I freaking love my life, or I want to end it. The meds keep me in the neutral zone."

"Thank you for writing this. When I read PostSecret this week, I was thinking about what my secret would be if I sent one in. My secret is that even right now, while I'm doing pretty well, sometimes those thoughts show up out of nowhere about jumping in front of a bus or thoughts assessing the effectiveness of using the nearby building or knife for suicide. I haven't told my husband—haven't even told my therapist. I thought it was wrong and this shouldn't be happening while I'm feeling well, and then I saw this article. Maybe now I will risk being vulnerable enough to talk to my therapist about it and work on it."

15 | Bipolar Disorder and Hobbies

The definition of a hobby is an activity done regularly in one's leisure time for pleasure. There is a problem with this for me and folks with bipolar disorder.

~

As someone with bipolar disorder, I can't tell you how many times I have been told that a hobby would be good for me. I took this to heart for a while. I have started many hobbies. Most I have done for about five minutes each.

The definition of a hobby is an activity done regularly in one's leisure time for pleasure. There is a problem with this for me and folks with bipolar disorder.

First, doing something for pleasure is great. The hard part is that when we are depressed, pleasure is elusive, if it is accessible at all.

When I have started a hobby and then stopped doing it because I was depressed, I felt guilty for not following through. The guilt then makes it harder for me to get back to the hobby after I have recovered from the depression.

On the other end, when manic and doing a hobby, I get obsessed by it. It is all I can think about. My mind always comes back to the hobby. I do the hobby. I think about the hobby. I dream about the hobby. I neglect everything else to do the hobby. My friends and family get sick of hearing about my hobby.

Eventually the mania subsides. But the negative, out-of-control feelings are still fresh in my mind and associated with the hobby. So doing the hobby feels bad.

The other thing about the definition of hobbies is that a hobby is something you do in your leisure time. Trust me; there is nothing leisurely about my life when I am manic. My mind is go, go, go. Slowing down to do a hobby is not an option.

There is a time when I think I can start a hobby and follow through. It is the time when I am stable. I know, however, that this stable time is only temporary. It is a serious decision for me to decide to do some-thing knowing the guilt I will feel for quitting it when I get depressed.

I also have the residual feelings from having obsessed about other hobbies and them playing a role in my mania.

I am not trying to say that hobbies are not good. For many, many people with bipolar disorder, a hobby gives them peace of mind that is elusive to so many of us.

As I say all this, I would really like to have a hobby that I can do that will give me pleasure. I like pleasure. I wonder if I had a hobby, would it help me be stable? With this in mind, I looked up some ideas for hobbies on the Internet.

I found one that appeals to me. I am talking about napping. This is a hobby I can get behind. It is good for me. The rest is good for my cycles. It feels good. I look forward to it. I don't obsess about it, and I don't feel guilty if I don't do it for a few days.

On the list, they spelled it wrong. They spelled it "knapping." I thought it was the British spelling or something. Then I looked it up. Knapping is the shaping of flint, chert, obsidian, or other conchoidal fracturing stone through the process of lithic reduction to manufacture stone tools or strikers for flintlock firearms.

Wow! I don't want to offend any knappers out there, but I think I will stick with napping.

"Now I know it's not just me, thanks! Some hobbies I go back and forth to and from, like reading. I'll obsess over it and then not want to do it at all while depressed. Then I get manic and read like crazy again. I've never just read normally. It's like that with all my hobbies."

"I can definitely identify with all of the comments and experiences. I also feel guilty afterward because of all the money that I have spent on the hobby."

"Once again, Dave, I find myself relating absolutely to what you have written. Thank you for your insights and humor. Not only do I pick up hobbies when I'm manic (to desert later when I'm depressed), but I spend money on that hobby. Lots of money. And I obsessively accumulate things related to the hobby in great abundance. When the depression strikes, nothing I've made looks 'right,' and I'm left with bills and lots of unused hobby supplies."

"Wow, once again you are talking about me! I love reading your blogs as they describe me to a giant T. I used to love to play the piano before the full-blown bipolar kicked in about seven years ago. I started playing and singing when I was eight years old. I'm fifty-eight now, and I sold my piano last year because it was like a giant demon constantly calling out to me and mocking me constantly. I no longer played it because it was all or nothing with it, and during mania the playing would run my husband, dog, and cat up the wall!!

I would bang, not play quietly, for hours and sing to the top of my lungs! I had turned from being the quiet, church-piano-playing person to full-out 'what is that racket?' mode. When I was in a depressed mood, it would mock me constantly. I sold it to get it out of the house and to save my marriage! I really think napping is my hobby of choice. It's a lot quieter at least."

16 | Misreading Situations

People who I thought liked me at work didn't. In my personal life, people who I thought were my friends weren't.

~⁓

*B*efore coming under the grips of bipolar disorder, I thought I was pretty good at reading people and situations. I worked in sales and did pretty well. Even after being diagnosed, I thought I was still good at it. But over time, something changed.

Now looking back, I am embarrassed and cringe thinking of times when I was oblivious to what was going on around me. People I thought were my friends weren't.

For many years during my dark days, I couldn't work. For a long time it was all I could do just to be. It took all my mental energy to fight the racing thoughts and anxiety. I simply existed. Work was out of the question.

Over time, things improved thanks to help and medication. I didn't want to just exist anymore. I wanted to get out in the world. And I wanted to work.

I decided I was ready, so I started looking for a job that was part time and low stress. I knew I could not handle more. I wanted to work. It was a desire to try to function in the world. That is when I came across a job at Macy's.

I was hired and worked sixteen hours a week in the men's department for minimum wage. I worked there for a year and was proud of myself for doing it.

I worked with lots of people. There was a lot of turnover. When someone moved on, my coworkers and friends and I met after work for a going-away get-together at a nearby restaurant.

After a year, I gave notice. I got a job at NAMI doing peer support work. That is when I found out I had been misreading the situation at work.

For me, there was no going-away party, no congratulations on my new job, nothing. People I thought liked me and were my friends weren't. There were no good-byes. I simply punched out on the time clock and went out the door.

For a year, I misread people's relationships to me. I misread work banter as a sign of people enjoying talking to me. I thought I was respected at work. Not so much.

Today I look back and wonder how I could have been so wrong. I know, being bipolar, that I didn't open up to people and tell them about my illness for fear of rejection. People knew there was more to the story than I let on.

Besides that, I don't know. After I had been there for a while, I felt good. It was a success in a decade of failures and loss. I was outgoing, and I thought I was considerate and interested in my coworkers. I liked many of them. And I thought they liked me. I was wrong. And to this day, I feel foolish for misreading the situation.

I misread other people and situations as well. I had friends that disappeared from my life. Were they really my friends? No.

So today I am cautious. I check myself often to see if I am misreading a situation. To keep from being hurt, I don't expect too much. I have one very close friend who I know is a friend. Others I am not so sure about.

I know other folks with bipolar disorder who share similar experiences. We all misread situations. We all get let down and sometimes embarrassed and hurt. It sets us back. We are all doing the best we can to read the situation. Sometimes we just get it wrong.

Comments

"Your article helped me. The same thing happened to me, but I was fired. I thought they liked me and I was doing a great job. Of course I kept my BPD hidden like I always do. Now I am too scared to work. This experience is crippling me. You've shown me a better way. I hope I have the courage to try again."

"Hi, I changed jobs thinking things would get better, but it didn't, and now I'm sitting with a huge issue because they want me to resign. I don't know what to do anymore; my family is suffering. I have just come out of hospital for having ECT, and I don't know where to try to get another job or even if I should try, but financially I'm buggered if I don't work. In South Africa, things are hard. Sorry, just giving my two cents as I can't even talk to my family."

"I've done this too, especially with work colleagues. I've thought they were friends but then learnt that they were complaining about me behind my back. It's heartbreaking and leaves me feeling stupid and embarrassed."

"It's the bipolar dilemma: don't tell and lose friends and jobs or tell and lose friends and jobs. I usually choose the former because it hurts less."

17 | Bipolar Disorder and Bad Memories

Having bipolar disorder, I have way too many bad memories. I have a lifetime of them.

~

I have lots and lots of bad memories. And I have eighteen years of good memories. I wonder why I seem to only to be able to remember the bad ones.

Thoughts will trickle into my head. Some I totally ignore. Others I spend time with. It seems to me that I should be able to decide which ones I spend time with. But unfortunately that is out of the question. But most memories just slip in and out of my head.

Good memories happen. But for me, they happen without joy. It didn't use to be that way. I have a good memory of a good memory. That is, I remember daydreaming about happy things. When the good memories come, I try to hold on to them for as long as I can. But they lift into the mist after just a few seconds.

I think I get why we need bad memories. They help me remember my mistakes so that hopefully I won't make them again. (I'm still working on that part.) This makes sense. And maybe my good memories pass quickly so I don't spend all my time daydreaming about them and become lost in my head. So I dwell on the bad ones?

But this has to stop. My commitment today is that I am not going to dwell on bad memories. The question now becomes "how?" I need a reminder when I am in a bad memory so I can cut it short. I think a rubber band on the wrist could work. When if I snap myself, I will let the bad one go and think of something positive.

I am a person who sees the glass as half full. I think this may work. You don't? There is a flaw in the plan? Snapping rubber bands on my wrist is not as powerful as the memories in my brain? Drat! I have to come up with a new plan.

Mindfulness could work. Every time I think of a bad memory, I will say, "Ohm, ohm, ohm." That may not work if I am in the physician's office. He might think I have bipolar disorder. Oh, that's right; I do have bipolar disorder. And that is where this all started.

Having bipolar disorder, I have way too many bad memories. I have a lifetime of them. I have memories of loss and panic. I have memories of losing everything and moving out of our house and living in the basement of some friend's house. I remember being wracked by anxiety and filled with self-doubt. I remember being in the hospital psych ward and at home after and being completely overcome with guilt. The feeling was hellish and overwhelming.

I remember the one person who was rude in a day filled with nice people. Why is that? I do talks for mental-health-related groups. I also perform stand-up comedy through Stand Up for Mental Health Portland (Facebook at Stand Up for Mental Health Portland). These talks almost always go very well. Do I remember these? Not so much. I remember the one three years ago in February that didn't go well.

Tell me some of your best bad memories. And then let me know if there is one memory that keeps coming up over and over again. And if you have a way to get from bad to good, let me know.

Comments

"Wow! Right on target!"

"If one more person tells me to just keep my mind on other things and stay busy...I will scream in their face!"

"I'm dealing with the overwhelming bad memories and guilt for five days now. The severity cycles, of course, but losing my sis unexpectedly last week really was a setback. She was such an incredibly loving, kind, and spiritual woman. Attending the funeral and seeing family and 'friends,' who I know are biting their tongues while speaking to me—and I, trying to be gracious yet fully aware of the bad things they remember about me...the panic ensued full force and all of the worse symptoms that follow! Feeling ashamed and embarrassed, I made it through the service and burial without a blackout, then more guilt for being obsessed with my bad, fearful, and angry thoughts...when none of this occasion is about ME! So now I can have more bad thoughts and bad memories and guilt. I think it's going to be a very long week!"

"Thank you, Dave. I've been struggling a great deal with bad memory syndrome as I'll call it. I've let it become too debilitating—feelings of embarrassment and guilt are overwhelming. I close the shutters to keep out the light of life by living as a loner when deep inside I love people and I love the world. I just have to work on some strategies for putting intrusive memories in their place, so thanks again for the article."

"Thank you so very much. I now understand that this goes with the territory of bipolar. This is the first I've heard of it, and I thought I was alone. I have bad memories that feel horrid. I call them flashbacks that punch me. Increasing the meds helped me not feel so punched, but I still have the memories. They are of everything I ever said or did wrong that should have embarrassed me then, but I was too sick to see it. They come out of nowhere. They are like racing thoughts that I cannot control. Breathing fresh air helps. Mostly I try to stay distracted. My mind is like a bad neighborhood; I shouldn't go there alone."

18 | Oversharing

For many people, oversharing with folks at the wrong time and place leads to rejection and isolation.

~

It is beneficial to talk about our illness sometimes: with family, with peers, with friends, with counselors and doctors. But for many people, oversharing with folks at the wrong time and place leads to rejection and isolation.

Many of the comments to my last posts have been from people who find themselves at a social or family function talking about their meds and latest trip to the hospital. This is a good way to bring people down and leave the other person with nothing to say. Soon they excuse themselves and leave us standing there alone and feeling foolish and rejected.

Our bipolar disorder is often the main part of our lives. We live it every day, and it takes most of our time.

We don't have the ability to read a book or get out and see a movie.

Oftentimes we also see ourselves as advocates for folks with mental illness. Because of this, we think we need to self-disclose and educate everyone we talk to. Again, there is a time and a place for this. But we need to recognize where we are and who we are talking to.

Here are five tips on how to avoid oversharing:

First, think about the event we are attending and who will be there. Ask ourselves, "Is this the place to talk about my mental illness, and how well do I know these people?"

Second, if this is a family function, only one person whom we are close to may want to know how we are "really" doing. Everyone else may want to talk about the latest movie or how our family is doing. They don't want to discuss heavy topics. It brings them down.

Nothing can stop a conversation quicker than oversharing about our mental illness and what meds we are taking and what side effects we are having.

Third, visualize talking to people. Think ahead about what we have to talk about that others might find interesting. Think about the topics so we are informed. And then practice.

This may sound odd. But visualizing a conversation and practicing what we are going to say is a huge stress reliever. Practice in front of the mirror. And, very importantly, practice smiling. People love to be around people who smile.

Fourth, practice listening. People love to talk—and mostly love to talk about themselves. Listening is an underused skill that is a major key in having a satisfying and mutually rewarding conversation. A lesson I learned long ago is that when having a conversation, smile, ask questions about what the other person is saying, and listen. By just doing this, we will have successful conversations.

And last, plan! Plan on what time we will leave the house to get to the event. Plan on what time we will arrive. Give ourselves plenty of time to get there.

Plan what we are going to eat and drink. Plan what time we are going to leave (a bit early is better than being the last one there).

Plan what we are going to talk about and with whom. But we can always be open to talking to new people about new things.

Plan on learning new information. This gives us a purpose to talk to people without oversharing about ourselves.

These tips help us reduce stress, which is one of the major byproducts of social functions for people with bipolar disorder. Instead of fearing the event, we can attend with a plan that we are comfortable with.

Practicing and visualizing give us the experience we need to relax and have a good time. Using these tips helps us from having panic attacks and meltdowns.

Instead of fearing someone coming and talking to us, we are ready. We know what things we want to talk about. We smile, ask, and listen. And we don't over-share. When we do this, the other person has a nice time talking to us. They may even become a friend.

Comments

"Thank you, Dave. I relate to much of what you have written about. My bipolar has become a fixation in our lives so much that we (as a family) forgot how to live life. This is slowly changing, but it all began with information like this. Yes, I have a mental illness. Yes, I am open about it and believe that society needs to hear more about the effects it has on individuals, yet for me, I learned I needed to pull back. Isolation already hurts, and when you realize that you are doing it unknowingly to yourself, it is a harmful reality. Times are improving for me and my family. We are learning together how to live again. PS: I also find humour helps!"

"I dread going places, etc. The planning I can do, but it's hard for me to be open. I have awkward social skills. But when I get comfortable, I start opening up. And I feel like I have to share everything, and I end up alone. I have other mental disorders, bipolar, anxiety, PSTD, and so many trauma experiences that I really feel alone, but with these tips, I might not feel alone."

"This is a great article. I tend to overshare a lot. I hear myself doing it, and though I want to stop, it's like a flood. Once I get started, it just keeps going. I have learned recently though that simply listening and asking people questions about themselves is the easiest way to take the focus off myself. Before I know it, time has passed, and the function is over, and I've barely had time to talk about myself. And that is a very good thing.

I leave feeling like I've met and learned about a great new person, and they tell me they really enjoyed meeting me as well. It's a great way to practice a little humility and selflessness, however small of an act it may be."

19 | Constant Conversations in My Head

I am having a constant conversation with myself in my mind. And by constant, I mean every minute of every hour of every day.

~

*H*i, this is Dave Mowry for *bp Magazine for Bipolar* vlog. Today I am going to talk about conversations I have with myself that are constantly going on in my mind.

A few nights ago, my wife looked over at me and said, "Dave, why are you so quiet today?" I said, "I don't know. Am I being quiet? I didn't realize." Then a few days ago, I thought about it and realized that I am having a constant conversation with myself in my mind. And by constant, I mean every minute of every hour of every day.

Thoughts will pop into my head, mostly negative, about experiences I have had. And I will have a conversation about this experience. Usually these conversations will last from ten seconds to thirty or anywhere in between. Then I'm off to another conversation for ten or thirty seconds and then back to the original.

Music helps. I listen to music, but I can never, ever, ever remember listening to a song all the way through. Somewhere, whether it be ten seconds or thirty seconds, a thought will pop into my head, and I will think about it and converse with myself about it. Then I will go back to the music. Then I will have a thought and go back to having a conversation with myself.

I meditate, and it helps, but it is not a solution. It gives me some quiet in between the thoughts because I will have a thought and start a conversation, and then I will let it go. Then ten seconds later, I am off to another thought. I go back and forth, back and forth, and back again. So meditation for me is only a slight, temporary relief.

Watching TV is helpful for me because I am focusing on something else. But the most relief comes from reading a book. I think—no, I'm sure—that everyone has thoughts that pop into their heads and conversations with themselves. I just wonder if my bipolar brain is the reason my thoughts are constant.

The next time my wife says, "Why are you so quiet tonight?" I will say, "Because I have been having a conversation with myself all day long."

I'm sure she is going to say, "About what?" Unfortunately I will have to say, "About everything and nothing." But by talking about it with her, I hope she will understand. And by talking about it, I will gain an understanding about these constant thoughts and conversations I have with myself.

Warm regards,

Dave

This is Dave Mowry for *bp Magazine for Bipolar* vlog. Bye, bye.

Comments

"Now I know it's not just me. The bipolar brain never stops going. Even in your sleep. It's excruciating."

"Omg feel better when I realize I'm not the only one with…sometimes I feel so lonely."

"This is me constantly. Insomnia rules my life right now thanks to my brain that lives a life of its own."

"I do this all the time. I didn't realize that other people do it too. In fact, just today I had to make a three-hour drive, and I did this constantly the entire time I was driving. I cried several times. Then I had to get myself back on track to remember that I was going to visit my grandchildren, and we are going to bake Christmas treats, and life is good."

"Oh my goodness, I just love your articles because they helped me know I'm not alone. I am a big fan of mindfulness, and I use mindfulness to help me when I get stuck conversing with myself, particularly about sad things. I also meditate like you do, and it is very helpful. I hadn't thought about music, so I'm going to try that as well."

20 | Panic Attacks: My Constant Companion

The sweat began on my forehead. At first there were just small beads of sweat, but soon sweat was running down my face. My armpits were being soaked. People were looking at me. I had to escape.

~

I have written about panic attacks before. Panic attacks are humiliating, embarrassing, and devastating. They are pervasive for those of us with bipolar disorder. I think it is important to write about this topic again.

For me, the panic attack lasts anywhere from minutes to hours, depending on the circumstances. My recovery from panic attacks takes days.

One of my earliest memories of a panic attack happened during my freshman year of high school. I was in algebra class. I liked algebra and was good at it. I liked my teacher, who was also my football coach, and he liked me.

One day he wrote an easy equation on the blackboard. I knew the answer immediately. But then there was trouble. My teacher called me up to the board to solve for x. As soon as I got to the board, my mind went blank. I began to sweat, and my heart was pounding. My eyesight blurred, and I froze.

After what seemed like forever, he took the chalk from my hand and asked me to sit down. He called someone else up, and they solved it immediately.

I felt embarrassed and humiliated. The rest of the class period was a blur. I could not process what was said. What was written on the board made no sense. I was in shock.

It took four days for me to be able to look at my teacher. I wasn't called on for the rest of the semester. I was thankful for that.

There were also the recurring times when I was back at college after a long absence. I thought I was well enough to take classes. Many of the classes were big, and that was OK because I could be invisible. But other classes were smaller. And one was especially challenging.

This was a sociology class I loved, with a great professor. I was early in my recovery, and when I went into class, I sat in the back corner so that only the side of me was exposed. Again, I tried to be invisible. I was OK until the professor broke us into small groups.

My heart beat faster, my breathing became shallow, and fear overcame me. It seemed like such a simple thing. No one else appeared nervous. *Why me?* I thought.

The sweat began on my forehead. At first there were just small beads of sweat, but soon sweat was running down my face. My armpits were being soaked. People were looking at me. I had to escape. I stood up and quietly left the room. I headed straight for the bathroom. I looked awful. My shirt was soaked. My face was so pale that I looked like a ghost.

I couldn't go back into the room while other people were there. I couldn't be seen like this. I waited in the bathroom until class was over and then went back in and got my bag. I slinked out of the building to the safety and seclusion of my car. I sat for an hour before I decided to try to drive. Home seemed a million miles away. I was so shaky that I didn't know if I was going to make it.

One of the hardest things I have ever done in my life is to go back to that class. I knew the panic attacks would happen again, and they did—almost daily.

That class taught me a lot. It taught me that I could face any challenge, no matter how embarrassing, humiliating, and painful. It taught me I could recover. It taught me to leave the room at the first signs of a panic attack. And it taught me that I was stronger than my disorder.

I hope that sharing my experiences is helpful. And you, by telling your story of panic attacks in the comment section and sharing how you deal with them, will show others that they are not alone—and that maybe, just maybe, there is help and hope when living with panic attacks.

Comments

"Thank you for sharing your story, Dave. I have severe panic disorder that I've thankfully been able to keep under control, but I'll never forget my first panic attack or these hundreds that followed until it got under control. It came out of nowhere!! I was doing my normal Tuesday night thing, which was watching my daughter during her rec cheerleading practice with the rest of the moms and some dads. I went to get up off the floor, and I suddenly got dizzy, and everything seemed unreal. Suddenly I had a body-warming rush of fear that went from my feet up to my head. I honestly thought I was getting ready to die! My brain was fuzzy because nothing felt real. I remember telling my daughter to sit in the middle of the backseat and strap her seatbelt right, but I don't remember us going to the car. I had to drive us home, which was about five miles away, but I had to drive slowly in case I died while I was driving and wrecked the car so my daughter stood a better chance of not being seriously or fatally injured (didn't have a cell phone back then). I prayed repeatedly to God to 'Please let me just make it home to tell my son and husband that I love them before I die. Please.' When we got home and inside, I was in complete fear mode. I KNEW the moment I told my family I loved them that I was going to take my last breath. I couldn't bring myself to say the words. I could feel the blood flowing fast through not only my veins but my capillaries in my entire body! Finally I demandingly said to my husband, 'Call nine one one now. I think I'm about to die.'

"I've been able to find something that I can do that helps me get through tough ones that I still get once in a while. I go to the happy, beautiful island I created in my mind. I focus hard on the sounds I'd be hearing on the island and the wind blowing as if I'm right there on the island. I remember a time when I wanted to die because I was having more than five panic attacks in a day, and some of those lasted for a few hours. I'd fear the next one so much that I'd send myself into one. I couldn't win."

21 | Mental Illness: A Balanced View

Another takeaway from the panel is that being rigid in our beliefs and expectations can cause us to get stuck in a bad place. To adamantly oppose meds or talk therapy or exercise or meditation causes us to get stuck in our bipolar brains.

～

I was on a panel discussion this weekend at a conference about different treatments for bipolar disorder. This was one of the best panels I have participated in. No one had a hidden agenda. All that the other panelists cared about is what works for folks with bipolar disorder. Here are my takeaways.

My first takeaway is that no one thing works for all people with bipolar disorder. The most common comments are that meds can be an important part of a treatment plan. But meds alone are not the answer.

Sometimes our med provider gets it, and we work as a team to improve our lives. Many times, though, we need more than our med provider.

A counselor who gets it makes a big difference in our quality of life. Maybe the most effective is a well-trained peer support specialist. Peer support specialists have walked a similar path as we have. They get it. Sometimes we only share our whole story with a peer. We know there is understanding without judgment.

Alternative treatments discussed were exercise, meditation, and supplements. Using supplements should always include being well informed about effects and conflicts with the person who prescribes your meds. Discussion of these with your doctor is recommended.

Exercise helps most people. We release endorphins when we exercise, and that helps our feeling of well-being. However, I have a friend who is consumed with feelings of anxiety during exercise. She feels good after. But during exercise, the effect on her mind is negative.

Meditation also helps folks find peace of mind and is a relief from anxiety. I have meditated for decades. When I am in the grips of anxiety, when I need relief the most, I can't meditate. My mind is racing with so many negative thoughts and noise that even meditation won't quiet it. I feel like a failure at meditating. Sad, huh?

What I have learned is that I have to be taking my antianxiety meds to quiet my mind enough to meditate. This is a time in my life when Western medicine and Eastern philosophy come together.

Too often, in the grips of depression from our bipolar disorder, we just can't do it. We just can't exercise. We just can't meditate. We just can't talk to someone. Our illness has us in its talon grips and won't let go.

Another takeaway from the panel is that being rigid in our beliefs and expectations can cause us to get stuck in a bad place. To adamantly oppose meds or talk therapy or exercise or meditation causes us to get stuck in our bipolar brains.

Worse is to try to influence others to take a treatment path because of a bad experience we have had or to intimidate someone into giving up something that helps.

My experience is that when someone says, "You have to try this. It's better for you," they are operating for their own self-interest and not for mine. That said, I'm tired of random people trying to fix me. What gives them the idea that because I have bipolar disorder I need their treatment expertise? Please don't tell me what I need to do for my bipolar depression and anxiety.

After the panel discussion, folks came up to us and commented on how nice it was to be part of a discussion that was informative without being stressful and combative. No one was made to feel guilty about choices they had made up to this point. And everyone received balanced information they can use to make decisions in the future. It was a day well spent.

Comments

"Thank you, Dave. I love your article (blog). I'm also bipolar. I'm now sixty-five years old. I don't feel that old. Everybody else just looks so young! There are people in my life that want to know what they can do to help when I'm depressed. Sometimes I don't know what to tell them. But it angers me when someone tells me what to do so they can fix me! And then there are those who walk away completely because my bipolar embarrasses them. I don't need those people in my life. But how can I tell someone how they can help when I really just want to be alone the times that I don't want to see anybody, or talk to anybody, or do anything? I know they mean well, but they don't help by not respecting my wish to work it out myself."

"I know the stigma attached to having bipolar, but there are good ways to counteract it. Like the post says so wisely, take your meds (the side effects will get better over time), see a counselor (I see my counselor every few weeks even if I feel good or normal—it is good to just check in with someone who won't judge), and then find something you enjoy that brings you back to center."

"What a difference a balanced view can make in our lives. We don't give up while trying to find what fits for us. Having a balanced view is a gift we give to others as they make choices that are best for them."

22 | Don't Disrespect Me because I Have Bipolar Disorder

Having bipolar is hard. Preparing for and going to meetings and appointments is hard. I respect you for the effort and energy you invest. I expect you to respect me too.

～

My appointment here at the coffee shop is at 9:00 a.m. I gave myself extra time to get ready to make sure I am on time. Being bipolar, I don't know which me is going to wake up or how hard it is going to be to get ready.

Today was a tough day. Getting up, I felt sluggish and unmotivated. It took extra time to wake up and get my brain going. I didn't want to get dressed, but I knew I had to. I made a commitment. Getting here on time was tough, but I made it.

I get my coffee and sit down, expecting my appointment at any moment. It is 8:55 a.m. I know she will be here anytime. After all, it was her who set the appointment place and time. I wait anxiously.

At 9:00 a.m., I start to think that I must be at the wrong place. Am I sure this is where she said to meet? Do I have the right coffee shop? Is today the right day? Do I have the time wrong? My anxiety goes up, and I feel really uncomfortable.

And then, at 9:10 a.m., I get a text. Fortunately, I have a smartphone. It's her. "I can't make it today. My dog is sick. Can you make it tomorrow? Same time, same place? Sorry."

After all the effort it took me to get up and get ready and the enormous anxiety that this appointment and waiting caused me, I feel let down and disrespected. Saying sorry at the end of her message means nothing. It is a throwaway word with no sincerity.

She must have known her dog was sick before our appointment time of 9:00 a.m. An 8:15 a.m. text—better yet, a call—would have felt like she took me into consideration. But to text me ten minutes after our appointment was set to begin is extremely inconsiderate and rude.

I finish my coffee and head home. It's a half-hour drive. "Can I meet tomorrow?" she asked. Hell, no. It took all my energy to get up and prepare to meet today.

Her apology was meaningless. Next time we meet, if we meet, it will be me who sets the time and the place. And I will tell her a meeting time that is half an hour early so I know she will be on time. Or if she cancels again, I will get the notice before I leave the house.

Has this happened to you? I am sure it has because it happens to me all too often. How did this become OK? And these are people who know I have bipolar disorder. They should understand the negative impact that has on me.

So what would you like to say to these people? How would you like to react? In the moment, we tend to not know what to say or get flustered. But thinking about it, here is what I would have liked to say:

Stop doing this. It is not OK to cancel an appointment less than half an hour before it's time to start. It is just plain rude and inconsiderate. You made a commitment. Fulfill it. I am more valuable than that, and my time is more valuable than that. "Sorry" doesn't cut it.

Having bipolar is hard. Preparing for and going to meetings and appointments is hard. I respect you for the effort and energy you invest. I expect you to respect me too.

Comments

"Dave, there is comfort in realizing that very few people without bipolar disorder would be able to blow off such a slight. Such rudeness and lack of empathy from anyone to anyone is dismaying at best. It says a great deal about the perpetrator's values and character. It is all the harder to bear for someone as sensitive as bp folks, of course. The remedy proposed for 'next time'—if there is a next time—is outstanding!! Thank you for this one—anyone at all to whom such a cavalier 'sorry' has been handed can gain practical insight from this anecdote."

"Thank you for the article. Made me realize once again that I'm not so alone in what seems to be a very disrespectful world!"

"It came to my attention last week that me and my 'illness' were being discussed among my fellow colleagues at work. I found e-mails where they point out all my weaknesses and how most of it is because I have bipolar disorder. I've had this strange feeling the last month that they were trying to get rid of me because I have bp. When I saw the e-mails, I knew I was right."

23 | Identity Theft: Take Mine

For years, I did not know who was going to wake up in the morning: the bipolar manic me, the depressed me, or the stable me. It seemed my identity changed daily.

～

For forty years, I have lived with bipolar disorder. I have seen all sides of it. For many years, I was in the grips of it without medical care. For much of this time, I did not know who I was.

For years, I did not know who was going to wake up in the morning: the bipolar manic me, the depressed me, or the stable me. It seemed my identity changed daily.

The manic me had energy and optimism. This is the me who started successful businesses. I was outgoing and presented myself well, which helped with the successes.

The depressed me had no energy and was full of self-doubt, dread, and pessimism. This was the me who lost businesses and hundreds of thousands of dollars in the process.

There was the stable me. I saw things for what they were. This me saw the ravages from the bipolar me and felt the regrets. I still had enough hope to think things would get better. And in time, they would—until the bipolar me woke up the next time and took over my life.

It was the manic me who did all the things that led to anxiety, embarrassment, and guilt. While manic, I had no filters. I would say the wrong thing. I would flirt with the wrong person (my eldest daughter's adult friend). I fantasized about a never-attainable lifestyle. And I would brag about my successes without mentioning my failures.

The anxiety would inevitably come. Soon I was filled with dread. Fear controlled my life. Normal challenges would be blown out of proportion, and my mind raced. Oh, how it raced.

I wanted so badly to be the same well person every day. I wanted to see the reality of things and not the unrealistically amazing or the unrealistically depressing.

Why couldn't I have the same identity day after day? Why did the bipolar play with my brain to create these three distinct people?

Bipolar manic: optimistic and outgoing

Bipolar depressed: hiding in the shadows and suffering in silence, afraid to let anyone see me, and overwhelmed with paralyzing anxiety

The stable me: the me who was so tired of being the other two and who had to pick up the pieces

If a cop yelled, "Stop! Identify yourself," I would say, "It's me. No, me! No, me!"

In the depths of the illness, I am sure others would welcome the identity thief. "Take mine. Take mine." But then who would we have left?

Comments

"I really connected with what you wrote. The stable me is oh so tired of picking up the pieces and finding new ways to move forward. But forward I go. Thank you."

"This sounds exactly like me. I have different 'personalities' as well, Becky, Sarah, and Sybil—Sybil of course being the worst; that's my manic episodes. For me, the changes happen clear out of the blue with no warning. I'm on a cocktail of meds that seem to keep me stable except for Sybil; she definitely is the hardest to tame. Thank you for sharing your story. It's always nice to hear from others in the same boat."

"I had many sides to me. Most often I was manic me, spending, racing, running, cleaning. Depressed me didn't get out of bed for days. And the well me had to explain behavior all the time. Well me was not present very often. This went on for over twenty years. Lots of medication, therapy, side effects, doctors' appointments, lost relationships, financial hardship, and the list goes on. When I finally got a grip on this disease, I wasn't really sure who I was. And neither was anyone else. Today I am strong, healthy, independent, and I like who I am. Unfortunately, because this is relatively new, I am not always received amicably. For as long as I was unbalanced, people knew how to react. Now I am not in need of being taken care of, and that is not always an easy thing to accept. People are afraid of the 'crash.' With time, it will get easier. Once people get to know the real me, I feel that all will be the way that it was meant to be."

24 | Peer Support Works

I listened intently and encouragingly. And as I did, folks would open up and tell their stories. Many times they were telling their whole story the first time. Never before had someone with a mental illness who had the tools to listen and to help, and who had shared experiences, been there to listen.

～

*P*eer support is where a person with a mental illness is trained to support another person with a mental illness. During my four years as a peer support specialist for the National Alliance on Mental Illness Clackamas County, Oregon, I met with over eight hundred peers.

Often a peer or a family member would call and make an appointment. The call to me at NAMI was often a call of last resort. The peer had seen a counselor and/or a psychiatrist. These sessions had not resulted in what the peer and family were hoping for. It seemed there was no real help.

Meeting with a peer for the first time, there was immediate acceptance. I made it clear that I wasn't a counselor and that I wasn't there to judge. I didn't take notes. I just listened. I told them that I have bipolar disorder and fought my demons for years. I was just someone who has some shared experiences.

Then I started to listen. I listened intently and encouragingly. And as I did, folks would open up and tell their stories. Many times they were telling their whole story the first time. Never before had someone with a mental illness who had the tools to listen and to help, and who had shared experiences, been there to listen.

More than once I had a suicidal person come in on their own or at the request of a friend or loved one. I would simply say, "Tell me what's going on." From there, they talked. Knowing they were talking to someone with shared experiences, they talked about the hard things. They talked about suicide.

One person, I will call him Fred, came into the office. We introduced ourselves briefly, and he said he was told I could help him. It quickly became obvious that he was terribly depressed and suicidal. I asked him if he was thinking of committing suicide. He said yes. Then I asked him if he had a plan. He did. And finally I asked if he had the means. He did.

I told him he needed to go to the hospital and asked if he was ready. He said he was. I asked if he had a ride, and he did. I called ahead to the hospital and let them know he was coming. I told Fred what to expect. I helped Fred find the words to use to describe what was going on.

Fred was in the psych unit for two weeks. When he was released, he came to me and told me I saved his life. He said that his previous plan was to go home after seeing me and end his life. The moment we met was his lowest point. My training and experience as a peer support specialist were exactly what he needed.

A trained peer support specialist knows that the meeting, the conversation, is not about them. And as we listen, folks tell us things that they have never told their counselor or psychiatrist for fear of being judged.

The relief washes over them, and they visibly relax. They talk more comfortably about hard times and embarrassing things. They talk about things they are guilty about. As they talk about their lives with bipolar—discrimination, mistakes, and sometimes abuse—the weight lifts off them.

Living with the anxiety, guilt, and fear of bipolar disorder, we often suffer in silence. We are lucky if we have the chance to talk to one other person with bipolar disorder about shared experiences without feeling judged.

Peer support gives us that opportunity. It makes a huge difference to know we have been heard and understood. Most important is to know that we are not alone. Here is someone else who lives with bipolar, and they are making it. Sometimes that is just what it takes to make it through the day.

Comments

"Thank you, Dave, for sharing this. I wish there were such a system here in my country, Malaysia. I hope I can one day be a peer support specialist myself and help others who need help like us."

"Thank you for sharing your story. I am in the process of taking the peer specialist classes and hope to get a job at a local mental-health clinic."

25 | My Lost Years

The years in between jobs and in the depths of my bipolar disorder are my lost years. These are the years I could not be with friends and lost them. These are the years I was not present for my wife and kids.

(This is one of my favorite posts. The words flowed when I wrote it. After I wrote it, I felt I had faced a major issue in my life.)

～

One of the things that bothers me the most about having bipolar disorder is the lost years. When I was well and happy, I did well in school, well at work, and well in my personal life.

Unfortunately these times of being well are in the minority. More often were the times of anxiety, depression, and mania. More often was the searching for medical care, diagnosis, and the right medications.

I took some time to reflect on the years of my life from the time I was eighteen years old. What I found out was not a surprise, but it was troubling at a visceral level. It was also sad and depressing.

In my adult forty-five years, I have had eighteen good ones and twenty-seven years of fighting my demons, suffering in silence, and hiding in the shadows.

During the good years, I had good jobs and started and ran successful businesses. I made lots of money, which, of course, I lost during the bad years. In the good years, I was bright and ambitious and was rewarded. But those good years seemed to only last three years at a time.

After three years of success, the anxiety, depression, or mania would kick in and take over my brain. I would fight it. Yes, I would fight it hard. But the bipolar disorder was stronger.

After a time of being on the edge, I would slide into depression. My outgoing personality would disappear. My job performance suffered. The anxiety would be overwhelming. Management would notice.

I never got fired. When I was younger and working by the hour, my hours were cut until I quit. When I was older, I would get laid off. More often I would quit.

Why quit? The depression progressively got deeper, and with it the anxiety became overwhelming. I couldn't do the job, and that created more anxiety. I became overwhelmed with guilt.

Finally I was so ill that I couldn't leave the house. I couldn't function. I couldn't shower. All I could do to get relief of any kind that I had to have to survive was to quit. I always waited until I was way too sick and overwhelmed.

At last I would make the phone call and quit. Or I would go in in the morning and quit with no notice. Out of all my jobs, and I have had a lot, only a few ended well with me giving notice and leaving on good terms.

This produced more guilt, which created more anxiety, which created more depression, which sent me further into the darkness. I would make up stories in my mind as to what to tell people was the reason I was not working. So I would lie about it, which created more anxiety.

The years in between jobs and in the depths of my bipolar disorder are my lost years. These are the years I could not be with friends and lost them. These are the years I was not present for my wife and kids.

There have been twenty-seven of these years, including recovery time. That is 60 percent of my adult life that was lost. That is twenty-seven years of anxiety, guilt, fear, loathing, and lies, and the occasional bouts of uncontrolled mania.

That is also twenty-seven years of lost hope and struggling each day to look for reasons to get up and continue on.

I have been working part time since I have been better. I started with a part-time minimum-wage job at Macy's. Then I worked for NAMI as a Peer support specialist, and now I teach stand-up comedy to folks with a mental illness through a program called Stand Up for Mental Health. A year ago, I coauthored a book about the impact of learning comedy on someone with bipolar disorder. It is called *No Really, We Want You to Laugh*.

I know that some or maybe a majority of you also have lost years. I am so thankful for my good ones. But they don't "make up" for the bad ones. I miss them. I mourn them. It pisses me off that I have so many. But talking about it helps. Thanks for letting me talk about it with you.

"It's funny…I know exactly what you mean. My husband and I both have bipolar, and we have discussed the 'lost years' on occasion, and we realized that we were grieving for what we never accomplished, never did, the lost jobs, the lost time, the wasted opportunities, and botched precious memories. But after all these years together, we are learning to move forward, as hard as it is some days, and try to do what we can now. No, I will never be a doctor, and he will never be an engineer, so we try to help others and spread the word about opening up about mental illness. Education and communication help so much, and we realize that if we can help even one person, then we have accomplished much more than we ever thought possible. Thank you so much for sharing!"

"Our lives seem to have run similar paths. My bipolar produced deep, deep depression, and my lost years were spent in bed. Like you, I was successful in business, but then the downside was as dramatic as the upside. Now, with the right combination of meds, therapy, part-time work, and facilitating groups for people in the spectrum, there is hope. Thank you for sharing your story as it makes it easier for us to tell ours."

"Thank you for sharing what I am sure is just the 'tip of the iceberg' to your life story. I read it, and it was like reading my story. I am fifty-five, soon to be fifty-six, and have experienced many if not all of what you have mentioned here. It does help me a lot to know that I am not alone, not 'crazy.' Bipolar is real. It can and does ruin lives as well as takes life from us and/or we take ourselves out of life. I have battles in my head daily sometimes from one minute to the next as to 'should I stay, or should I go?' It seems there is no end, and life is a constant state of taking three steps forward to be followed by seven steps back, which only makes our state of mind worse. Thank you for sharing."

"Wow, you hit the nail on the head. I wasn't diagnosed until I was thirty-seven; I'm now forty-nine. I had thirty-seven lost years when I didn't know what was wrong with me but I knew something wasn't right. I lost job after job, friends, and two marriages. I am now trying to accept this diagnosis and go on with my life knowing that had I known years ago that I was bipolar, I could have changed the course of my life. It is so upsetting, and nothing will ever get those years back. Thank you for writing this."

26 | We Are Beautiful People: A Message of Dignity and Hope

For years, I didn't think I had a purpose. I was just existing. But then I found something meaningful.

~

The most beautiful people we have known are those who have known defeat, known suffering, known struggle, known loss, and have found their way out of those depths. These persons have an appreciation, sensitivity and an understanding of life that fills them with compassion, gentleness, and a deep loving concern. Beautiful people do not just happen.
—*ELIZABETH KUBLER ROSS*

For years, I didn't think I had a purpose. I was just existing. But then I found something meaningful.

I started working as a peer support specialist at NAMI, and I began to share my story. As I did, I began to make a difference, first in my life and then in others' lives.

In 2011, *The Oregonian* newspaper did an article on me. It was the first time I truly shared my story. The gist of the story was that most folks with mental illness are not dangerous but are neighbors and friends and family.

The response to the article was 80 percent positive. People called and wrote, saying that my story was their story. Many used it as a tool to have a conversation with family and friends about their experiences with bipolar disorder.

Sharing my story was and is an important part of my healing. I became an advocate for the mentally ill. Every time I shared my story, my bipolar illness had less control over me.

Like you, I have known defeat, suffering, struggle, and loss. I lost years of being present with my wife and kids. I lost friends. I lost peace of mind. I lost businesses and hundreds of thousands of dollars.

I know that being a public advocate for people with a mental illness and sharing my story has had negative impacts on my life. A simple Google search of my name followed by "bipolar" brings up several pages of hits. Anyone who does this search finds the good and the not so good.

Today I have found my way out of the depths. For people going through these struggles, I tell them there is help and there is hope. Because I have been through the struggles and the pain and the loss, I have the credibility to make a difference. But I had to go public to get the credibility.

For years, I wanted to live quietly with my experiences. I dared not tell anyone, thinking that their judgment of me would be negative and swift. And in many cases it was.

I recently wrote about suffering in silence. For most of us, that is an inevitable and necessary part of our recovery. But there comes a day to talk to others about our struggles. It is hard. But this is when our beauty shows.

When someone finds out they are talking to a person who has walked the walk of mental illness, they tend to open up—often for the first time. This openness can begin the healing. I tell my story so others can begin to tell theirs.

I remember the first time I heard someone talk openly about their mental illness. I got a feeling of calmness in my chest. I realized I was not alone.

Those of us who have experienced the madness and the loss and the pain and suffering have a deep understanding of the experiences and feelings of others. We are beautiful people.

Conclusion

Writing this book and re-reading the comments solidi-fied my belief that we folks with a mental illness are courageous, loving, and yes, beautiful. Our challenges make us stronger.

Whether we suffer from depression, anxiety, panic attacks, or bipolar disorder there is hope. There is an end to our dark days and lost years. We heal and that healing makes us productive, compassionate, loving people.

Share these stories with others who live with a men-tal illness. Share them with family, friends, care-givers, and others.

When you are ready, share your story. Share it proudly. Telling your story will help someone else, and when we help someone else, we help ourselves.

Kickstarter Contributors
Major Sponsor $500
Jeff Caton
Friend and Sponsor $100
Karen Bradley Mercer
Nicole Dalle
Vicki Raethke
Julie Fast
Friend and Supporter $50
Brooke and Ryan Dilley
Christopher Houghton
Tony Koo
Dan Bristow
Tara and David Rolstad
Gayathri Ramprasad
Cindy Becker
Steve Levine
Friend $25-$30
Martha Spiers
David Shannon
Wendy Sample
Chris Farentinos

About the Author

Dave Mowry is an author living in Happy Valley, Oregon, with his wife, Heather. He is also living with bipolar disorder, depression, severe anxiety, panic attacks, and more. Writing about his experiences has allowed him to reach out to others and build strength through empathy.

Mowry has also written *No Really, We Want You to Laugh*, a book about being a stand-up comedy teacher who caters specifically to those with mental illnesses. He and the other comics perform throughout the Northwest for audiences of thirty to four hundred people. He is also a certified peer support specialist and the cofounder and executive director of the non-profit mental health–focused Peer Wellness and Work Initiative.

Mowry has a BS from Portland State University. He also blogs for the bipolar-focused *bp Magazine*, in which many of his most popular articles can be found.

Made in the USA
Las Vegas, NV
07 March 2022

45220717R00090